THE RELUCTANT
ENTREPRENEUR

THE RELUCTANT ENTREPRENEUR

Turning Dreams Into Profits

MICHAEL MASTERSON

WILEY

John Wiley & Sons, Inc.

Published by John Wiley & Sons, Inc., Hoboken, New Jersey.

Published simultaneously in Canada.

For general information on our other products and services or for technical support, please contact our Customer Care Department within the United States at (800) 762-2974, outside the United States at (317) 572-3993, or fax (317) 572-4002.

Wiley also publishes its books in a variety of electronic formats. Some content that appears in print may not be available in electronic books.
For more information about Wiley products, visit our web site at www.wiley.com.

Library of Congress Cataloging-in-Publication Data:

Masterson, Michael, 1950-
   The reluctant entrepreneur : turning dreams into profits / Michael Masterson.
      p. cm. – (Agora series ; 73)
   Includes index.
     ISBN 978-1-118-17844-7 (hardback); ISBN 978-1-118-22727-5 (ebk);
     ISBN 978-1-118-24021-2 (ebk); ISBN 978-1-118-26492-8 (ebk)
1. Entrepreneurship. 2. New business enterprises–Management.
3. Small business–Management. I. Title.
  HB615.M3723 2012
  658.1'1–dc23

                          2012004737

Printed in the United States of America

10 9 8 7 6 5 4 3 2 1

This book is dedicated to the hundreds of thousands of people who read Early to Rise *from 2000 to 2011 when I was writing for it.*

CONTENTS

FOREWORD: IS THIS AN "INSPIRATIONAL" BOOK?

Most people go into businesses for the wrong reasons. And most people go about starting and developing businesses in the wrong way.

My friend Michael Masterson, whom I admire immensely, has done a phenomenal job of attacking myths and misinformation about entrepreneurs and how they actually create and grow successful enterprises. You will finish this book with a different, deeper, and more realistic understanding of what is really involved in getting a brand-new business going, getting traction for it in its marketplace, protecting it during its fragile infancy, and growing it to mature success. Getting a new business going is not easy. But it's not mysterious either.

In one of my own books, *No B.S. Guide to Business Success in the New Economy*, I make the point that most people uninitiated to and contemplating entrepreneurship are fearful about it and wonder if they are up to it, because of a belief that successful entrepreneurs are wild-eyed, daring risk takers, akin to riverboat gamblers frequently "going all in" with questionable hands. This is not true at all. Success is about smart risk management, not about wild risk taking. This is one of many concepts about business success where Michael and I have strong agreement—and where he can set you straight.

He also adeptly disabuses the reader of the need for The Big Idea, visionary innovation, and motivation as key success ingredients. Instead, he approaches business as a methodical sequence of good decisions.

My own 35 years of experience starting, buying, building, and selling businesses of my own; working intimately with many clients in developing businesses from the first baby steps to as large as $1.5 billion, but more commonly $10 million to $30 million; and acting as an advisor and coach to thousands more entrepreneurs has convinced me beyond any shadow of doubt that invention and innovation are vastly overrated and methodical implementation is more important. That more entrepreneurial fortunes revolve around the use of known, proven processes for advertising, marketing, sales, management, and finance applied to a good idea than are born by the new, radical, revolutionary, romantic Big Idea. That being a visionary is not required and not necessarily even helpful—instead, that being able to improve on already proven products, services, and businesses offers the best opportunity. (Disney didn't invent the amusement park. DeVos and VanAndel with Amway neither invented soap nor multi-level marketing. Schultz and Starbucks didn't invent the coffee shop. Zappos neither invented shoes nor e-commerce. I didn't invent newsletters.) That motivation matters, but that motivation without great clarity about a sound, sensible, progressive plan of action leads only to frustration. That successful entrepreneurs are extremely pragmatic.

Michael Masterson impresses me as a committed pragmatist. His advice, this book, is simply and purely about what works. In the real world. With startups.

He and I both come from the disciplined world of direct-response marketing, where measured results rule and nothing else matters, not even our own opinions. In that world, you learn to test as cheaply and harmlessly as you can, toss aside the unproductive and underperforming quickly and unemotionally, and find and leverage what works. This is experience that academic theorists do not have, that traditional brand and image advertising "creatives" shun, that many small businesspeople never embrace. But when every dollar matters, as it does with startups, this is the approach that trumps all others—and you will come to appreciate it via this book.

None of this suggests trepidation. It suggests prudence.

I actually take exception to the word "Reluctant" in this book's title. "Timid" might have been a better choice. But even that seems unfair. Perhaps "Cautious"? "Methodical"? Had I been asked to name this book, I might have chosen "The Pragmatic Entrepreneur." Pragmatism is about finding out what works and doggedly doing it, to the point of resisting distractions and disparate ideas. It's about focus. About well-organized effort.

You can draw a lot of confidence from this—so that you are not reluctant. You can have confidence in process.

The most valuable and sustainable businesses on earth are built on and driven by great processes. McDonald's consistently outperforms all other fast food purveyors not because they have better tasting or healthier or more interesting products. They have the best process. A company I study and own stock in, Tupperware, led by a CEO, Rick Goings, that I admire, is thought of by the public as a purveyor of unique plastic food containers and kitchen gadgets. But Tupperware's success is so much more about process than product. Of its six core competencies, only one has to do with product innovation and manufacture. The other five are processes—for recruiting sales agents who will work on commission and recruit and train others; for interesting people in hosting in-home parties; for conducting successful in-home sales parties; for managing a multi-tiered, global sales organization of independent, part-time agents; and for managing the financial aspects of marketing and growth.

The business I began very humbly, now GKIC, serving tens of thousands of small business owners and entrepreneur members, operating local chapters, publishing six newsletters and numerous online and home study courses, conducting large conferences, and delivering complex business coaching programs, is certainly fueled by great content and information, but is driven even more by sophisticated processes—such as for marketing through thousands of affiliates; for the intake and conversion of new, trial members; and for developing and presenting extraordinary events. One of the most valuable things to be gained from Michael's book is a grasp of the power of process and the guidance for developing your own business's processes.

Candidly, this is not the most heart-stirring and exciting business book ever birthed. It is not rich in hyperbolic passion. It is factual. Accurate. Straightforward. Based on real, hands-in-the-dirt experience creating and growing not one but a number of multimillion-dollar companies. Do it once, you have a great cocktail party story. Do it repeatedly, you have a formula, a system. And that's another thing I'm very fond of and focus on in my books: system. Learn from Michael the criticality of system. Utilize a great system—you'll have a great business.

Few would, at a glance, call this an inspirational book. But, ultimately, there are two ways to be inspired. One is by the charismatic dynamo, the lofty thinker, the stylish orator, the grand and glorious—if vague—idea. All too often, this produces only castle-building in the clouds of imagination. The temporary inspiration and excitement wanes as you come to realize that there's no foundation and no instructions for building one. This is how being inspired turns to being intimidated. The other kind of inspiration, the kind that has always worked for me and for my clients, is rooted in scientific, formulaic, systematic approaches to problem solving and opportunity monetization. Knowing what must be done and being able to work with and on a scheme for achieving well-defined objectives is more sustainable inspiration. On that basis, Michael Masterson has produced a deeply inspirational book.

In the realm of business literature, he has definitely produced an important book.

DAN KENNEDY
www.NoBSBooks.com
www.DanKennedy.com

Dan Kennedy *is a from-scratch multimillionaire serial entrepreneur, author, and publisher, and a trusted strategic advisor, marketing consultant, and direct-response copywriter for entrepreneurs and their companies spanning more than 200 different product, service, industry, and professional categories.*

ACKNOWLEDGMENTS

I'd like to thank Starr Daubenmire, for her work in tracking down facts and information and helping craft each chapter; Jason Holland, for his help in keeping this project moving; and Judith Strauss, my editor, for her efforts to make my sentences clear and comprehensible.

THE RELUCTANT
ENTREPRENEUR

INTRODUCTION

Entrepreneurship: What It Is . . . and Isn't

When Mary Kay Ash decided to start her own business, she did it the hard way. She quit her job, cashed in her savings, and invested everything she had in an idea that some called "crazy."

The odds were overwhelmingly against her. She had to overcome obstacle after obstacle. But she triumphed. Today, Mary Kay Cosmetics is a billion-dollar company.

Hugh Hefner's path was similar. He financed his crackpot idea for a men's magazine by talking 45 skeptical friends and family members into lending him money. And like Mary Kay, he struggled for years before making it big.

We love stories like these because they are so inspiring. But they are also misleading. They perpetuate the myth that to become hugely successful you must be willing to risk everything—your money, your reputation, even your close relationships.

In fact, most successful entrepreneurs got to the top by taking a very conservative approach.

THE REALITY OF CALCULATED RISK

Take Bill Gates. Legend has it that when the entrepreneurial bug bit, he dropped out of Harvard to start Microsoft. A serious gamble.

But, as Rick Smith tells us in *The Leap*, Gates didn't drop out at all. He took an approved leave of absence. Then he relied on his parents' financial support while he developed his programming skills and made contacts. If it hadn't worked out, Smith argues, Gates would have gone back to Harvard, finished his degree, and made a good living as a corporate executive.

Gates had his family behind him. He also had a Plan B. He was not then, nor is he now, a person who takes extreme risks.

Another example is Ben and Jerry. Contrary to popular belief, their entire startup was driven by risk avoidance.

Their initial idea was to get into the bagel business. But when they realized how expensive the equipment would be, they looked for something else. Turns out, it was cheap to make ice cream. So they rented a vacant Vermont gas station and started to sell fresh, handmade ice cream to the locals and tourists.

At first, they barely covered their costs. But they knew they had a really good product. And by putting in lots of hard work, they gained ground. After two years, they began to sell their ice cream to local eateries. And it was only after those first wholesale efforts paid off that they thought about expanding beyond their backyard. They went statewide and then national.

Then there's Wayne Huizenga. He started Waste Management with a single garbage truck that he drove himself. He bought his second truck with profits he made from the first, and the third with profits from the second. Eventually, he grew the business into a billion-dollar enterprise.

Dell, Apple, and Google—three of the most successful businesses of the last 20 years—were started by people with big ideas but very little money. In dorm rooms and garages, financed by pocket change instead of venture capitalists, they pursued their dreams. Only after their businesses were up and running did they gradually take on investors.

These were smart, sensible people who believed in what they were doing. They were willing to invest time—lots of time—and their own money. And they spent that money very carefully. Yes, they took a risk. But it was a calculated risk.

THE RELUCTANT ENTREPRENEUR

This is a book about entrepreneurship—a collection of strategies that will help you start and grow your own successful business. But it was written specifically for people who are nervous about doing it. Maybe even a little afraid. People who don't have the guts to quit their day jobs and risk their futures, no matter how excited they are about their business ideas.

In other words, it was written for "reluctant entrepreneurs" like me.

I started my business career as a reluctant entrepreneur, and I'm still one. Along the way, I have grown dozens of multimillion-dollar companies. One grew beyond the hundred-million-dollar mark and another one is even bigger than that.

These days, I work as a consultant. As part of my job, I give advice on marketing and product development. But what I enjoy most of all is the hardest thing to accomplish . . . and that is getting a brand-new business going.

Without question, the first two stages of business growth—from zero to $10 million, say—are the most challenging. It is relatively easy to turn a $10 million business into a $50 million business. But taking a company from zero to $1 million and from $1 million to $10 million—that takes more than smarts and hard work.

At this point in my life, you might think I would want to consult only with the bigger companies, since growing them is easier. (And there are times when I wonder if I'm a little crazy for not doing it.) But I can't resist the challenge of starting from scratch. I love identifying a promising idea, having other people tell me it can't be done, and then making it work.

That is what really motivates me. It's not the money I can make. (I have enough of that.) And it's not the glory. (As a consultant, I'm almost always invisible.) It's the sheer, egotistical, irrational delight I get by proving doubters wrong.

LAUNCHING A SUCCESSFUL BUSINESS TAKES MORE THAN MOTIVATION

There is a science to entrepreneurship, but it is not rocket science.

Every successful business begins with a good idea. Then you have to make a series of smart decisions—big ones and smaller ones.

In prior books—and especially in *Ready, Fire, Aim*—I have argued that the typical business goes through four stages. And that each stage presents the entrepreneur with distinct challenges and opportunities. I identified those challenges and opportunities. And I suggested ways to meet and take advantage of them. In my humble opinion, *Ready, Fire, Aim* is the best book ever written about starting and building a business from nothing to more than $100 million.

This book is different in two ways.

First, I am going to focus only on the first two stages of business growth—from zero to $1 million and from $1 million to $10 million.

Second, I'm going to back up to an even earlier stage of entrepreneurship—when you are still a "would-be" business owner. I am going to describe, in detail, how to break through the fears and doubts that may be holding you back. And if you don't yet have a good, workable idea for a business, I'm going to show you how to come up with one.

If you have ever dreamed of starting your own business but have been afraid to try to turn your dream into reality . . . this book is for you.

If you have ever had an idea for a new business but figured nothing would come of it because you didn't have the time or resources to develop it . . . this book is for you.

If you have ever simply wanted to add an extra stream of income to your current salary . . . this book is for you.

Most startup businesses fail as the result of making a handful of stupid mistakes. In this book, you will learn what those mistakes are . . . and how to avoid them.

IT'S OKAY TO BE CAUTIOUS

As I said earlier, I've started and grown dozens of multimillion-dollar companies. But I've done it as a reluctant entrepreneur. I have never started a business *entirely* on my own. Nor have I ever invested my life savings—or even a fraction of that—in any business.

And yet, I have succeeded. Over and over and over again.

This book lays out the way I've done it. It is not meant to be exhaustive. I will focus on the most important things I've learned. The secrets that have worked repeatedly—not only for me but for my protégés and clients. I will stick to the fundamentals of entrepreneurship, as I understand them—fundamentals that apply to almost any business in any business environment.

I will help you design your new business, make rational decisions as you go, and reduce your risk to a minimum while increasing your chances of success.

As I said, entrepreneurship is not rocket science. We will build your business like a simple go-cart. We'll plan it out, collect the parts, and put them together. I'll show you how to test your go-cart even before we build it. And we'll make sure you don't spend all your lunch money on it.

SUCCESS IS NOT A ROLL OF THE DICE

I am not a betting man. Gambling, I believe, is only for people who don't care if they lose. I do care. And I'm sure you do too.

I started my first business because I wanted all the benefits of entrepreneurship—the independence, the prestige, and the money. But I've never been willing to risk much to get those benefits. In other words, I wanted my cake. And I wanted to eat it too.

That's why I call myself a reluctant entrepreneur.

I honestly believe that if I did it, you can do it. Why? Because I am anything but your typical businessman. I don't have a business degree and I've never even taken a business course. But I know exactly how to structure a business and make it succeed. (That's why my clients pay me handsomely to consult with them on their multimillion-dollar businesses.) And I am putting it all down in this book as the ultimate guide for entrepreneurs.

AND ONE MORE THING . . .

You know that starting a new business is going to require an investment of time. You know it will require some money too. You do it because you hope there will eventually be a financial payoff. But there's more to it—benefits you might not expect.

For one thing, there is tremendous satisfaction in charting your own course and seeing it through. And when you employ other people, you create wealth not just for yourself but for them as well.

Think about it. With their small businesses, entrepreneurs create jobs and have a significant impact on the economic growth of the entire world.

Entrepreneurs make a difference. They touch people's lives.

It's as simple—and profound—as that.

I'm looking forward to welcoming you to the club.

CHAPTER 1

───

WHAT, EXACTLY, IS A RELUCTANT ENTREPRENEUR?

Philip Knight has a net worth of about $11 billion. That makes him the twenty-third-richest person in the United States, according to *Forbes*.

If you don't recognize his name, you wouldn't know how he made his fortune. He didn't inherit it. He didn't develop an Internet technology. And he didn't make it trading derivatives.

He made his money as an entrepreneur.

When most people encounter the word "entrepreneur," they think: "Risk taker. Rule breaker. Someone very different from me."

There is a good reason for this. The media has long portrayed the entrepreneur as the daring visionary, willing to sacrifice almost everything to realize his dream. Whether it is about one of the great industrialists—such as Carnegie, Rockefeller, or Mellon—or a modern-day example like Ray Kroc or Victor Kiam, these are the stories that capture the public's imagination. These are the stories that sell.

And there is some truth to it. Ray Kroc, the founder of McDonald's, famously said, "If you're not a risk taker, you should get the hell out of business."

Victor Kiam, president and CEO of Remington Products, put it this way: "Entrepreneurs are risk takers, willing to roll the dice with their money or reputation on the line in support of an idea or enterprise."

But not all entrepreneurs approach business with such reckless abandon. Some take a more conservative route.

That brings me back to Philip Knight . . .

PHILIP KNIGHT'S STORY

In the late 1950s, Phil was a middle-distance runner on the University of Oregon track team. At the time, American track shoes were made from little more than reprocessed wastage from tire companies. A new pair cost only five dollars. But it didn't last much longer than a single, five-mile race. Phil customized his track shoes as best he could, and was somewhat successful at getting better traction and durability.

Later, while in graduate school at Stanford, he took a course in small business development. One of the assignments was to invent a new business. Remembering his experience as a college athlete, Phil came up with the idea of making and selling superior athletic shoes. To keep costs down, he would manufacture them in Japan. (It was a lot cheaper than doing it in the United States back then.) And he would then market his shoes in competition with Converse and Keds and other popular American brands.

I don't know what grade he got on that assignment, but I'm guessing it was pretty good.

After graduate school, Phil traveled to the Far East. In Japan, he was drawn to the athletic shoes he saw in department stores. He was especially impressed with the Tiger brand. So, on impulse, he made a call to the head of the company. He told him about his bad experience with American shoes. They met to discuss a potential business deal. And soon thereafter, Phil was given the right to distribute Tiger shoes in the western United States.

While waiting for his samples to arrive, Phil got a job as an accountant. He also taught classes at Portland State University. But despite the project he'd completed in graduate school, Phil realized he didn't know anything about marketing athletic shoes. So he spent his spare time learning as much as he could about the business.

By the time the samples arrived a year later, he had written a business plan and made several key contacts in the United States. One of his contacts was Bill Bowerman, the legendary University of Oregon track coach. Phil hoped Bowerman would give his shoes an endorsement. But Bowerman did more than that. He agreed to become Phil's partner.

The two men formed Blue Ribbon Sports on January 25, 1964, with a handshake agreement. They each invested $500 of their own money in the venture.

For the next five years, Bill worked on improving the design of their shoes and Phil sold the Japanese imports out of the trunk of his Plymouth Valiant at track meets across the Pacific Northwest. Meanwhile, both men kept their day jobs. Neither one risked their savings or gave up their salaries. Little by little, they built their little startup into a profitable small business with 45 employees and sales of about a million pairs of shoes a year.

That's when they changed the company's name. Phil's first idea—Dimension Six—was roundly rejected. Then a friend, Jeff Johnson, suggested a name that had come to him in a dream. It was the name of the Greek winged goddess of victory: Nike.

The rest, as they say, is history.

WHAT WE CAN LEARN FROM THIS . . .

The success of Nike is legendary. And sometimes, in telling the story, business writers depict Phil Knight and Bill Bowerman as archetypical risk-taking entrepreneurs.

As you now know, nothing could be further from the truth. If anything, they were cautious—even timid at times.

I am writing this book because the common perception of the entrepreneur never fit with my own experience.

I have started, co-started, or consulted on the creation of at least a dozen successful entrepreneurial businesses. Two of them were holding companies that launched dozens of smaller companies. And in my experience, the safest and surest way to develop a successful business is not to come up with a brand-new idea and put all your money into it. It's to start out slowly, like Phil Knight did. Develop your sources, contacts, and business plan first. And keep your day job until the new business is making so much money that you no longer need the salary.

HATCHING A BUSINESS WHILE YOU KEEP YOUR DAY JOB

The cautious approach to entrepreneurship has helped many of my friends and colleagues build seven-figure incomes. Not surprisingly, it figures heavily in my book *Seven Years to Seven Figures*.

A reporter for CNN Money was particularly interested in the concept. He had six basic questions for me. I'll go over them here because it presents the big picture. Then, we'll get into the details.

One: What does being a "reluctant entrepreneur" mean?

A reluctant entrepreneur is somebody who keeps his day job while he gets his ideal job going in the evenings and on weekends. He is willing to take the initiative to start his own business. But he's not willing to quit his current job and lose the income. The compromise he accepts is that he will have to work 60 to 90 hours a week for several years before he can either abandon his great idea or fire his boss.

Over the years, I expanded the concept to include employees of a company who, by virtue of extraordinary performance, earn their way into the position of managing a product or division that is their own. They are still employees, but they operate autonomously and share in the wealth they create.

I have been both kinds of entrepreneur . . . and I liked them both.

Two: What does it take to manage a side business while keeping your day job?

It takes discipline, faith, integrity, hard work, and a very understanding family. It's not easy to work a full day at the office and then go home to put in time on your own project. But if you create a plan and follow it in an orderly fashion, you can do it.

Three: What does it take to make a side business succeed?

Start a business you know something about—a business that is based on some interest you have. And take the time to learn about that business from the inside out. That might mean getting yourself some part-time work in the industry.

To succeed in any business, you must understand what kinds of products the marketplace desires and what price points are "sweet." You must know how those first sales are made—what specific marketing techniques are employed to generate a sale without spending too much money acquiring the customer. You must understand the back end of the business (how to upgrade a new customer into buying higher-margin products). And you must become competent at the basic business skills: marketing, salesmanship, and negotiation.

Four: What common pitfalls should be avoided?

There are several.

The most common is dictating to, rather than listening to, the market. New entrepreneurs often waste precious time and effort hoping to bring something brand-new and exciting to the marketplace. If the product doesn't exist, there is usually a good reason for it. So it's better to take a cautious approach to product development, too. Start off with a better or cheaper version of a product that has already proven to be in demand.

The next-biggest mistake new entrepreneurs make is spending too much time and money on non-essential pursuits. The fundamental activity of a business is the commercial transaction. Natural-born entrepreneurs know that their best chance of success comes when they devote 80 percent of their initial resources to making the first sale. Forget about buying business cards and copy machines. Figure out how to make that sale.

Five: Who is best suited for this approach?

Anybody who has modest intelligence and drive, tenacity, and integrity can do it. That's what's so nice about it. You don't have to have the moxie.

Six: When, if ever, do you have to choose between your two jobs?

That's the easiest question to answer. When your own business is up and running and bringing you more income than your paycheck, you ask yourself "Do I like running this business?" If the answer is "Yes," walk into your boss's office and tell him that you want to talk about transitioning out of your job. (As tempting as it may be to quit on the spot, you have to do this in a professional manner.)

MY FIRST ONLINE PUBLISHING BUSINESS

I had published and marketed information products before, but the first time I did it entirely online, there was a lot I had to learn. I didn't know anything about the Internet. Which meant I didn't really understand how the business would make money.

Knowing how a business will make money is the most important piece of information an entrepreneur needs. It is also usually discovered after the business is launched.

I decided to limit my investment to $50,000. That is a ridiculously small investment for a full-scale online publishing business. But I figured I could compensate for that with hard work and a team of talented employees.

It took two years for that business to reach the million-dollar mark, and another four years to reach $8 million. But the year after that it more than doubled in size and enjoyed revenues that were 10 times higher.

Along the way, we made many changes and improvements as we learned more about doing business online. Those improvements made our work easier and the business more profitable.

But if I had waited to start that business until I knew everything about the Internet, I'd still be waiting.

So the formula is this: Invest the minimum. Spend a reasonable but limited amount of time acquiring knowledge. And take action as soon as you can.

In other words, "Ready, Fire, Aim"!

Get ready by learning what you have to know to get started. Take action ("fire") by testing your business idea in the marketplace. And then gradually fine-tune ("aim") the business with what you learn after you're up and running.

In answering the six questions for the CNN Money reporter, I outlined my cautious approach to entrepreneurship, and the wisdom of keeping your day job as you start your business.

In *Ready, Fire, Aim*, my bestselling book on entrepreneurship (published by John Wiley & Sons), I covered the four stages of business growth. But in this book, I will focus only on the first two—getting your business from zero to $1 million and then from $1 million to $10 million.

I will begin by talking about what it takes to follow the "reluctant entrepreneurship" path—and why it's better than the alternative. I will also provide general guidelines that should work for anyone who wants to become successful without taking much risk. And I will tell you some of the most important secrets I learned about the very early phases of being in business.

In subsequent chapters, I'll tell you about the problems you are sure to encounter as your business grows. And I will offer solutions for every one of them.

THE MYTH OF THE "ENTREPRENEURIAL TYPE"

Many business books are written by academics who back up their theories with researched data, not life experience. These include prestigious titles published by Harvard Business Press, Stanford University Press, and Wharton School Publishing.

Still others are written by journalists who interview or study entrepreneurs. Seth Godin, author of *If You're Clueless About Starting Your Own Business*, is an example. Robert Kiyosaki, author of the hugely popular *Rich Dad, Poor Dad*, is another example. And I would add Tim Ferriss, the author of *The Four Hour Work Week*, to the list.

These authors have had modest success as businesspeople. But apart from their publishing empires, they've had little or no success in developing multimillion-dollar enterprises.

Writing about something they haven't done does not mean that their observations are invalid. But as a reader of these books, you have to wonder if their recommendations are trustworthy.

The question here is about risk: How risk-tolerant do you have to be to succeed as an entrepreneur?

And my answer is not very. For every entrepreneur who succeeds through boldness, I believe there are a dozen who achieve success by taking small, timid steps and learning as they go.

That's not the conclusion Seth Godin came to. In *If You're Clueless About Starting Your Own Business*, he tells us that these are the traits you must have if you want to be a success:

- A positive, committed attitude so you can stick with it through "change, insecurity, and indecision"
- A natural love of challenge so you will have the energy and enthusiasm to handle the demands you will face
- The ability to manage a lot of stress and work at a high energy level
- The willingness to take responsibility
- A preference for being in charge rather than following orders
- A sense of excitement and urgency about growth and change
- The ability to sell yourself and your business

I identified with some of these (the willingness to take responsibility and the preference for being in charge). But I wasn't sure about the other ones. Luckily, he provided a 25-question self-assessment test to find out if you have what it takes to be an entrepreneur. I took it—expecting to get a very high score. In fact, I scored only 79.

According to Godin, here's what my 79 means:

"You possess some entrepreneurial traits, but probably not to the degree necessary to buck the daunting odds. If your score on the last 15 questions was 15 or below (which mine was), your risk is even greater. Keep working for someone else."

Keep working for someone else? I gave that up 30 years and $50 million ago.

WHERE DO SUCCESSFUL BUSINESS OWNERS COME FROM?

Despite what some experts would have you believe, successful entrepreneurs are not the offspring of the privileged elite. Only 6 percent of *Inc.* 500 business owners were affluent when they began their careers. Fifty-eight percent were middle-class, and a very impressive 35 percent were either poor or working-class.

A colleague of mine—the guy who recommended Godin's book to me—scored very well on the test. And he is, indeed, a superbly confident risk taker. But he has not been able to build a business that lasts. He starts one. And because he is smart and aggressive, it works well for a time. Then it falls apart.

While I admire my friend's courage, I see his capacity for risk as a deficit, not an asset. In all other ways, he has what it takes: He is knowledgeable. He is responsible. And he has good management skills. But he jumps whole-hog into every new idea he comes up with—and that is his undoing.

So now, let me give you a different test. How many of the following statements do you agree with?

- I don't like to risk my money. Not at all.
- I would never think of quitting my job and risking my life savings.
- I like the idea of being my own boss, but I am not sure I would be good at it.
- I am willing to take responsibility for my actions—but I still don't want anyone to find out about my mistakes.
- I sometimes have good ideas but often have no idea what to do.

How'd you do?

If you agreed with most of those statements, you are a reluctant entrepreneur at heart. Like me. And I hereby invite you to join our ranks.

This book will show you how to create a successful, cash-flowing business without doing anything that makes you feel uncomfortable. You will start off taking baby steps. (Reading this book is the first one.) And you will move forward at your own pace.

You will not be required to risk your savings. And you will not be told to quit your day job. In fact, you will be prohibited from doing it.

I would argue that your chances for success are actually better because of your cautious nature. It will keep you from making many stupid mistakes. So embrace the fact that you like security and regularity and order. Those traits will serve you well in building a stable, profitable business.

If you are ready to get started, keep reading.

CHAPTER 2

THE FIRST
QUESTION YOU
MUST BE ABLE
TO ANSWER

Most would-be entrepreneurs are motivated by an idea—an idea for some great new product. But they almost never ask themselves the big question: Is this the kind of product I can actually sell?

Take John Ellis. He has an idea for a food product. He calls it "Esther's Health Soup" after his beloved late mother. She concocted a chicken-based vegetable soup for John's father, a man who hated vegetables.

John doesn't know what to do next. He talked to someone at SCORE (an organization that offers free advice to entrepreneurs). But he was told that it would take years (and lots of money) to gain FDA approval for his soup. So he has come up with some ideas about how to market the soup himself. And he wrote to me, wanting to know if they are good avenues to pursue.

"I'm a musician," said John in his letter. "I play at restaurants, catering halls, and country clubs. I am especially friendly with one caterer in my neighborhood. Would that be a good outlet?

Or should I approach a major company and sell my formula to them?" John also wondered if he should try to contact the original owner of Whole Foods Market, a family friend.

What can I say? John seems like a nice man. He makes his living as a member of a band. And he dreams of selling soup.

He loved his parents and wants to immortalize them by turning a soup his mother made into a commercial product. After reading a few books, he took the initiative to speak to a retired executive at SCORE. And he got a lecture on how difficult it would be to execute his idea.

I have always had mixed feelings about SCORE. I am sure many volunteers are formerly successful businesspeople (with a smattering of blowhards and ne'er-do-wells in the mix). But there is a fundamental problem with getting advice from people who have been out of their industry for two or three years: They lose touch with the market. Add to that hardening arteries and aching joints, and you have a non-profit organization filled with grouchy old naysayers.

John deserves better than he got at SCORE. But his ignorance of business is so profound, I'm not sure they could have helped him. Right now, his goals are purely sentimental. And a sweet dream to honor your parents just isn't the same as having a workable business idea.

John's greatest resource is the connection with the original owner of Whole Foods Market. Unfortunately, the guy is likely to be long retired. (And maybe working part-time as a counselor at SCORE, discouraging young people from doing what he did.)

But before John even considers contacting him, he needs to find out if his product is really as good as he thinks. By "good," I mean sellable. And he won't find that out by serving it to his friends. What are they going to say? ("John, I never wanted to say this when she was living, but your mom was a lousy cook.")

John's best bet is to start selling the soup at a local flea market or giving it away on street corners. No doubt he would be violating public health laws in doing so, but he probably won't get hauled off to prison. He could also look into getting a booth at a weekend greenmarket. Or he could approach a takeout place that features soup on their menu and see if they'll take his "on spec."

If Esther's Health Soup starts selling like hotcakes, John should write back to me . . . and then I'll tell him the steps to take next.

> *"In the modern world of business, it is useless to be a creative, original thinker unless you can also sell what you create."*
> —*David Ogilvy*

RULE NUMBER ONE OF RELUCTANT ENTREPRENEURSHIP

Don't even think about quitting your job until your business idea is proven and profitable.

There is only one way to find out if your product is good, and that is to start selling it. The sooner you start selling it, the faster you will know. (Most products, it turns out, are not as good as the inventor—or her son—thinks they are.)

That's a very important part of the reluctant entrepreneurship strategy. The strategy also includes:

- Deciding on a business to start. Don't fret that you might pick the wrong business. Just pick something.
- Getting an internship or part-time job in the kind of business you want to be in—in the marketing department, if possible. You will use this experience to learn everything you can about how that business sells its products. And if you don't have time for that . . .
- Allocating at least five hours a week to studying the industry you're interested in. Ten hours would be better.

Once you have a pretty solid understanding of how your future business works—how to source or create products, price them, and market them—you can get started in a small way.

YOUR INITIAL CHALLENGE: GENERATING POSITIVE CASH FLOW

Every business has a unique potential for success that is realized when all the key elements are put together in just the right way. Once you understand this formula, profits come to you reliably and regularly.

Initially, your challenge will be to generate as much positive cash flow as possible.

Let's say your business idea is to sell reading lamps through ads in the back of magazines. Your plan is to break even on the initial ad, and then sell additional products to the people who buy your lamps. You will do that by sending them a small catalog.

For such a plan to work, you would need to test various ads in various magazines. Then you would have to continue placing ads in those magazines while you fill your orders. In the meantime, you would be sending out your catalog to bring in more sales. The money from those sales would give you the cash flow to keep going while you fully and completely test your business model.

We'll talk a lot more about marketing in Chapter Seven. The point I want to make right now is that in the beginning, you should focus on your highest-margin efforts. That is to say, you should continue placing ads only in those magazines that produce above-needed response rates for you. In this case, that would be the ones that generated more than enough cash to pay for the ads. Maybe enough to cover your order fulfillment costs and leave something to pay for the catalog mailing.

Later, after you have established a reliable source of cash flow, you can begin testing lower-margin (but potentially more profitable) marketing schemes.

EDUCATING YOURSELF ABOUT BUSINESS

The difference between successful entrepreneurs and those who fail is usually a question of which ones figure out the way the business works before the money runs out.

You can minimize the problems if you begin with the maximum amount of knowledge. The best way to do that is to start a side business that is a knock-off of one you've worked in.

In addition to that, you have to become smart about business in general. Here are some ways to do that:

- Read the business press voraciously but efficiently. You don't need to spend more than 30 minutes a day on this. But you should spend that time and you should be selective about your reading. You'll want to focus on books, articles, and essays that pertain to your industry—primarily the how-to pieces. Give preference to authors who've done it themselves as opposed to academics or journalists.
- Supplement your reading by going to seminars and attending conferences. Person-to-person contact is invaluable.
- Take meaningful correspondence courses. When you find a good home-study program that pertains to your field, don't hesitate to invest some time and money in it.

If you pay attention to the marketing—your first and most necessary job—and continually improve your product and service, your side business will grow. In two or three years, it should be big enough to hire you as the CEO. Then, and only then, can you quit your day job.

Once you become CEO, things should really skyrocket. You'll be able to devote all your time and energy to this one single enterprise. And the benefits of all that concentration will pay off in terms of a big payout when you're ready to retire.

CHAPTER 3

WHAT IT TAKES TO BE A SUCCESSFUL RELUCTANT ENTREPRENEUR

Louis Borders had proven that he could start a successful business. The bookstore he'd founded with his brother Tom in 1971 had become a national chain, Borders Books.

Then, in the late 1990s, Louis's entrepreneurial juices started flowing once again. He decided to start another company. No longer actively running Borders Books, he had plenty of time. He also had loads of money. And he believed he had a great idea: an online home-delivery grocery service. He called it Webvan, and there was nothing "reluctant" about it.

With his connections, he was able to raise all the startup capital he needed as well as convince high-profile businesspeople to sit on his board. The only thing he didn't have was experience in the supermarket industry. But that didn't faze him. He was fearless.

The first thing he did was spend a billion dollars building warehouses. Next, he bought a fleet of delivery trucks. Then he installed dozens of high-end computers and server systems. And he hired several thousand people, including hundreds of senior executives to run the business. He lured them in with big salaries, tantalizing bonuses, and luxurious office spaces. He spared no expense. The chairs they sat in were Herman Miller Aerons, at almost a grand a pop.

It looked like he had done everything right. There were glowing reports in the financial press about his likely success. Investors were dying to buy stock in Webvan.

Then reality set in.

Consumers weren't as quick to change their shopping habits as Louis thought they would be. The assumption behind the business—that people would choose convenience over time spent going to the grocery store—was wrong.

Louis built it, but they didn't come. And since the profit margin in the grocery business is so slim, Webvan began losing big money immediately. Week after week, the losses piled up. When Louis finally called it quits, 2,000 people lost their jobs.

Louis Borders was an experienced businessman. In starting Webvan, he did everything first class. But he didn't do the most important thing an entrepreneur must do before going forward with a new venture: He never tested his idea.

Had he tested his idea, he would have discovered that people like to shop for groceries. They enjoy going to the market. They like to walk through the aisles and browse. And they love to find things on sale that they frequently use.

Not to mention the fact that most people like to squeeze their own tomatoes before buying them.

Louis could have tested his idea by making a deal with a distributor and marketing groceries in a few sample locations. He would have found out quickly and inexpensively that his core concept was flawed. Had he done so, he would have saved himself and his investors a fortune. And he might have then used his extensive resources to test another idea, and another . . . until he found one that worked.

Marty Metro was another entrepreneur who jumped into a business feet first. His idea was to buy gently-used cardboard boxes from large companies and resell them at bargain prices. He was confident he would make millions.

He invested his life savings in the business. He bought truck-loads of boxes and advertised them for sale. The response was enormous. Customers clamored for the boxes, and Marty was jubilant. Sales were great—but profits were non-existent. In fact, he was losing money. And he didn't know why.

After three years, frustrated and $300,000 in debt, he gave up. His mistake, he now knew, had been to launch the business before he'd factored in the delivery costs.

He had been fearless but would be fearless no more. He had proven that his idea was marketable and he wanted to give it another try. But this time, he would do it as a reluctant entrepreneur.

First, Marty got a job so he could support himself. Then he studied successful business models that might work for him. He realized he needed to partner with a delivery company so he could control those costs. And after landing a deal with UPS, he market-tested his new business model in Los Angeles. He did everything on a shoestring budget until he saw positive results.

Today, Marty Metro is founder and CEO of UsedCardboard Boxes.com, a multimillion-dollar company.

Marty's advice to new entrepreneurs couldn't be clearer: "Don't start a business until you are sure it makes money! Make sure that you have a great business plan before you waste your (or anyone else's) time."

"The cautious seldom err."

—*Confucius*

THE RELUCTANT ENTREPRENEUR IS A SMART ENTREPRENEUR

The reluctant entrepreneur wants to build his own business and become wealthy one day, but he wants to do it cautiously. He knows that however good and exciting his business idea seems to be, its profit potential is unknown until it has been tested in the marketplace.

He is ambitious and hopeful but not foolish. He realizes that he has only a limited understanding of the market he is entering, and he does what he has to do to compensate for it.

As Louis Borders and Marty Metro learned, confidence and the willingness to take a huge risk are not the keys to entrepreneurial success. What you need is a healthy dose of anxiety, a good day job, and a step-by-step plan for getting your business off the ground. The anxiety will keep you from spending all your money before you've given your business idea a fighting chance. The day job will keep food on the table while you test your business model. And the step-by-step plan . . . well, this book will help you create that plan.

FIVE BAD REASONS FOR WANTING TO START YOUR OWN BUSINESS

1. *You're currently out of work.* Don't start a business just because you think it will be easier than finding a job. You'll be spending resources precisely when you should be conserving them. You'll feel compelled to move along faster than you should. You won't want to take the time to really test out your marketing strategy. Desperation is a lousy motivator. It leads to mistakes that can result in total failure.

2. *You don't want to work for someone else.* I know this sounds contradictory—but even if you're the boss, you're still working for someone else: your customers. And that can be more demanding than any job.

3. *You want to work fewer hours.* Eventually, you may get your business to run pretty much without you. But that's

not going to happen for a long, long time. In the beginning, you can expect to spend even more hours on your business than you would on the typical nine-to-five job.

4. *You don't like to deal with people.* No one builds a multimillion-dollar business without dealing with people. You need to recruit and manage an entire team. You need to market your product to a wide audience. And guess what? They're all people.

5. *You're looking for easy money.* If your only motivation for starting a business is to get rich quick, you're in trouble. You'll be facing many obstacles and challenges before you reach your goal. Will it be worth it? Absolutely! Will it be quick and easy? Absolutely not!

THE FOUNDATION OF YOUR BUSINESS: SIX STRATEGIC CHOICES YOU HAVE TO MAKE AT THE VERY BEGINNING

Not all businesses are created equal. Some require a great deal of capital investment. Most manufacturing businesses, for example, require millions of dollars just to get started. Others, such as developing a successful social web site or board game, require more than money and time. They require a certain amount of luck. It's like becoming a pop singer or actor. You can have a great product (or skill) but your marketplace is simply too competitive.

So how do you decide on which business to get into?

Pick an Industry You Know

There's no better foundation than building on what you know. You might be drawn to the rush of something new and exciting, but your chances of success decrease with every step you take away from what you're familiar with.

Say you have a successful neighborhood restaurant called The Steak House. Your basic business is selling a certain kind of eating experience to the community. Over a few drinks with friends, you come up with two new business ideas:

1. The first is to open a local restaurant called The Fish House.
2. The second is to go into the wholesale steak-selling business.

Both of these businesses have several elements that relate to what you are already doing. The Fish House is almost identical except for one difference—you will be selling fish, not steak. All other key aspects—how you attract new customers, how you create a profit margin, and how you control your costs to deliver a bottom line—remain the same.

Starting a wholesale steak-selling business is about selling steaks. And that's what you do. But in this case, there are many differences. For one thing, the market is different. You are not selling to local diners but to regional businesses. This means the selling strategy is different. Which means the profit margin is different. And so on.

Opening The Fish House is an example of starting a new business that is only one step removed from what you know. Opening a wholesale steak business is three or four steps removed.

The first business has a good chance of succeeding. The only unknown: Will there be a big enough local market for fish? The second business has a poor chance of succeeding. There are simply too many things you don't know about it . . . too many inside secrets that are blocked from your view.

It is possible to succeed by going two or three steps away from your core experience. But as a rule, you want to take one step at a time.

Starting from scratch, learning a new skill, and gaining experience takes time. The danger is that you'll become overwhelmed and quit. The learning curve is just too steep. But if you choose something you already have experience in, you've already got one foot in the door.

BEWARE OF THE CONCEIT OF OUTSIDE KNOWLEDGE

One of the most common mistakes made when choosing a business to get into is thinking you know things you don't.

For instance, you might enjoy reading. You read at least one book a week. You love buying books, owning books, and talking about books with your friends. It only seems natural that your passion for reading would lead to opening a bookstore of your own . . .

The problem with this thinking is that you are going on what I call "the conceit of outside knowledge." Your experience, vast though it may be, has been as a customer, not a business manager or owner. Your experience *feels* deep and certain. But it isn't.

In addition to bookstores, businesses that typically fail due to this mistake include:

- Restaurants
- Vacation tour operations
- Bed and breakfast enterprises
- Art galleries
- Gift shops
- Antique stores
- Coffee shops
- Sports-related businesses

(continued)

> **BEWARE OF THE CONCEIT OF OUTSIDE KNOWLEDGE**
> **(*CONTINUED*)**
>
> If you're tempted to start a business in a field you have never worked in, be aware that much of what you do in the beginning will likely be wrong. Ask yourself if you have the resources—human, capital, and emotional—to push the business forward after you've made those mistakes.
>
> Be advised that when you enter an entirely new field, you are not expanding on experience. You are *starting over*. If you still have the urge to go with one of these businesses (which I do from time to time), go back and read this section again.

Pick the Right Product to Sell

There is absolutely no need to try to invent something new. In fact, that is a very bad idea. Entrepreneurship is not a case of "build it and they will come." If nobody else is selling what you want to sell, there is almost certainly no market for it.

What you want to start with is a product that is already working for other marketers. One with a proven track record. And there are many to choose from.

You have to be impressed with the variety of businesses that are alive and thriving. Look over any list of the fastest-growing small companies and you'll see things like tax services, professional cleaning products, insurance, adult day care, computer hardware, telecommunications, waste management, IT staffing, and more.

One retired guy I know manufactured those brushes that are inside glue jars. Another imported sunglasses from Asia. Another imported and sold oversized bronze statues from the Philippines. These are not real estate, oil, or software barons, but they are all very rich.

All over the country, thousands of obscure businesses are operating. They employ hundreds of thousands of people. They quietly make their owners millions of dollars.

That doesn't mean every business has the potential to make a lot of money. There are plenty that have all the cards stacked against them.

How can you tell? Look around at the owners of businesses that are similar to the one you're considering. If they have been working at it for seven years or more and are still driving used cars and living in small houses, it's probably not going to work for you.

Forget trying to become the next Facebook or YouTube. They get all the glory when the media shines a light on entrepreneurs. But that kind of instant success is akin to buying a lottery ticket. Most likely, you'll be working nights and weekends to get your startup business off the ground. That's the hallmark of a reluctant entrepreneur . . . to stay within the safety net of a regular job. To have benefits and a steady paycheck until you know your idea is feasible and will make you some money.

Like I said, you're always better off starting with something you know. A product you're already familiar with. It must fill a need that already exists in the marketplace. But—and this is more important than you might think—it must also be something that interests you. You are going to be married to this idea. You are going to be sacrificing time and investing resources into it. If you are not keenly and seriously absorbed by the whole concept, you won't last long. You won't be able to maintain the momentum it takes to go through the process of developing and running a multimillion-dollar business.

Pick a Way to Add Value to Your Product

Your business idea can come from anywhere. It can be the result of a disappointing experience with a product you bought. It can be a flash of inspiration when you realize how much more useful a service you've been using for years would be if it were modified ever so slightly.

It must, as I said, be based on something other people are already selling profitably. But you need to make it better in some way. You need to add enough value that it will prompt your prospective customer to pull out his wallet and pay you for it.

How can you do that?

Nick Swinmurn, the founder of Zappos, did it by taking a familiar product (name-brand shoes), adding convenient online shopping, and topping it off by overwhelming his customers with extraordinary service.

One example: Zappos has a 365-day return policy with free shipping both ways. They also upgrade customers to expedited shipping—without telling them they're going to do it. Customers expect their shoes to be delivered in three to seven days. When the shoes show up on their doorstep the next day, they are more than impressed.

No surprise that 75 percent of Zappos's sales are from repeat business and referrals. The result? Almost $1 billion annually.

Pick the Right Way to Market Your Product

Every business has two sides: product development and marketing. Many would-be entrepreneurs have good product ideas but they know nothing or next to nothing about marketing.

Learning how to sell your product is your single most important job as an entrepreneur. The sooner you can figure out how to acquire customers, the sooner you will be able to quit your day job and live the life you are dreaming about now.

Of all the forms of selling, the strongest by far is direct marketing—online, in the mail, and in magazines and newspapers.

You don't have to sell face-to-face to be a great direct marketer. You can learn the skills at home in your spare time. You can learn them by taking correspondence courses. And you will get all the fundamentals by reading this book.

Marketing is such a big topic that I will be devoting a whole chapter to it. For now, recognize that the way you market your product is one of the core strategic choices that will be the foundation of your business.

Pick the Right Offer

Once you have developed your lead product, you must devote 80 percent of your time and attention to making your first profitable sales. By that I mean sales to your target audience. That will happen with the right offer. Friends and family do not count. Your mother or sister may rave about your product and think you are a genius, but the buying public determines your success. When you're selling to them, you are really in business.

You must also understand the back end of your business. You must learn how to convert new customers into repeat buyers. You must learn how to turn a $50 purchaser into one who has a lifetime value of $100 or even $1,000. All of this will happen with the right offer (or offers).

This is not a static thing. Marketing offers change over time, even if the basic principles do not. I'll be giving you examples of those basic principles.

Pick the Right Way to Get Your Marketing Copy Written

This is where a lot of entrepreneurs drop the ball. They think they can write their own marketing copy. Copywriting, however, is a particular skill that involves not just writing but the art of persuasion.

Did you get a renewal letter today for any magazines you subscribe to, perhaps offering a discount or free gift? How about an offer from a bank for a new credit card? (You're prequalified and eligible for super-low interest rates!) Maybe a local merchant is having a sale this weekend and invited you to come by.

All of those pieces were written by copywriters.

Hiring a copywriter is no small responsibility. Make the right choice and you get great copy that brings in sales by the bushel. Make the wrong choice and you end up pouring thousands of marketing dollars down the drain.

Eventually, you will want to have a really good copywriter on staff. Still, I strongly urge you to try your hand at it yourself. Later in this book, I'll get you started.

IT'S NOT ROCKET SCIENCE

Starting your business by making these six strategic choices will get you off on the right foot. From there, it is simply about learning the necessary skills and avoiding the most egregious pitfalls.

Some experts would have you believe that entrepreneurs are born, not made. I am not in that camp. I believe that if you have a well-thought-out marketable idea . . . and you're knowledgeable about how to grow that idea into a money-making enterprise . . . your business will thrive.

As I've said before, you don't have to be a risk taker. As a reluctant entrepreneur, your cautious nature will be one of your greatest strengths. It will help you avoid the most common mistakes. So embrace your cautiousness and believe in this approach. It has worked for dozens of people I've mentored and I'm sure it will work for you.

Marty Metro's story at the beginning of this chapter is a prime example of what I'm talking about. Marty had a great idea. It was very marketable. But with his first try at turning it into a business, he went down in flames. With his second try, he did it as a reluctant entrepreneur. And then he was finally on his way to a multimillion-dollar success.

CHAPTER 4

HATCHING THE NEW BUSINESS: OVERCOMING FEAR AND TAKING ACTION

Liz McKinley was working for an oil refinery in Kansas. She had been hired as a pipeline scheduler but quickly learned the business . . . and began to dream of starting her own company.

Liz was smart. She kept her day job, saved as much money as she could out of her salary, and kept her eyes open. After a few years, she identified a niche in the market that she thought she could expand upon. Liz noticed that petroleum companies tended to be third- and fourth-generation family-owned businesses. They usually covered a fairly narrow region because they worked with their own fleet of trucks. It dawned on her that she could service a much wider area by outsourcing the trucking.

Liz had $100,000 in savings. She wasn't sure how much it would take to start her business, but she certainly didn't want to risk it all. She had twin toddlers at home that she had to support. Liz just didn't know if the time was right for starting her own business.

Then something happened that shifted Liz into high gear. Her father died suddenly. Around the same time, one of her close friends died too. Liz was struck by how quickly life can pass you by. She realized that she had some money . . . she had some know-how . . . and she had a good business idea.

Was she scared? Sure she was. But that didn't stop her.

Like I said, Liz was smart . . . and cautious. She did not go out and rent expensive office space or buy fancy equipment. She began her company from her own home. She juggled business with taking care of the twins. It made for some long hours. She often caught up on paperwork at night after the kids were in bed. But Liz's business, Pinnacle Petroleum, grew from those humble early days in 1995 to annual sales of $130 million.

As bestselling author Seth Godin points out, most people who buy books on entrepreneurship never get beyond the dreaming stage. They are reluctant to get started, he says, because deep down inside they don't think they have what it takes to succeed.

I think this is true. I have spoken to thousands of would-be entrepreneurs. I've noticed that when I ask them what they're waiting for, they all have the same answer. "I'm not quite ready," they say. "I'm going to start next [fill in the blank] after [fill in the blank]."

A well-known business coach once told me, "Fear is a major obstacle for would-be entrepreneurs. They will use any excuse to avoid taking action. Most of the time what they do is simply buy another book on how to start a business or sign up for another course."

I didn't like it when he said that to me 10 years ago. I had just started my Internet publishing business, and business advice was my main topic. I wanted to believe that my readers were going to jump on my recommendations and put them to work immediately. But I soon realized that he was right.

I've already pointed out that a healthy dose of fear is a good thing. It makes you cautious. And that will keep you from making many stupid mistakes. Just don't let it keep you from taking any action at all.

> *"The way to get started is to quit talking and begin doing."*
> —*Walt Disney*

YOUR FIRST THREE ACTION STEPS

From the very beginning—as soon as the entrepreneurial itch strikes—there are three action steps you can take to start turning your dream into reality.

1. Find the time to do it.
2. Find the money to do it.
3. Get yourself up to speed.

Finding the Time to Do It: Time Management

As a fledgling entrepreneur, you will become a five-to-niner. What is that? It's someone who works a regular nine-to-five job—and then focuses on his own business from 5 to 9 P.M. Or from 5 to 9 A.M.

That's a lot of hours. You will need a system to keep yourself on track . . . and keep yourself from burning out. Part of that means carving out time for family and fun, too. It's not just about work. You cannot expect to work all the time without recharging your batteries. You also can't expect to put in long hours without the support of your loved ones. (Never lose sight of what is really important in your life.)

There are lots of specific systems for managing your time. Find one that works for you. (I've included my own system in the Appendix to this book. You might want to start with that one.)

From the outset, you need to know how much time you are willing (and able) to invest. That will help you set realistic long-term goals. You have to break those goals down into monthly and weekly objectives. And if you find that achieving those short-term objectives is taking longer than you expected, you have to revise them accordingly.

It takes constant, determined effort.

Finding the Money to Do It: Financing Your Business

It's never too early to start looking for ways to fund your startup business.

Like Liz McKinley, you could use your own money. But it could take years to save up enough. Using OPM (other people's money) may seem like a much better way to go—but it can turn against you.

When you borrow money to start a business, you are putting yourself in a subordinate position. Because their money is at risk, your financial backers are going to hamstring you. They'll demand all sorts of restrictions and reporting requirements. And if things go badly, the very same people who believed so strongly in you can become your worst enemies.

Still, if you have huge capital needs, you may have to consider outside investors. And you can find them all over the place. An Internet search for "venture capital" or "angel investors," for example, will yield several good directories. One of those directories is put out by the National Venture Capital Association (nvca.org). You might also try: the U.S. Small Business Administration, your local Chamber of Commerce, local business incubator programs (often part of a local university or city/county/state economic agency), and your state government's economic development department.

Venture capitalists expect to see a significant return on their investment. So you will have to show them proof that your idea has a good chance of being profitable. This means you must provide them with detailed projections and up-to-date market data. And you must convince them that you (and/or your partners) have the experience to run a business. In short, before you even start to look for outside investors, you need a well-thought-out business proposal.

Get yourself a good guide on how to write a proposal. And while you're putting it together, keep this in mind: Your prospective investors are not interested in your mission or your big dreams. All they care about is how much money they can make.

My usual preference is to partner with people I have worked with before. These are people who have the resources to help me make a new business work. That kind of arrangement has resulted in my most frequent and greatest successes.

That said, there is one more idea to consider: getting your customers to pay for your product or service in advance.

It isn't every business that lends itself to customer financing, but it is possible much more often than you'd think. The trick is to show your potential customers how they stand to benefit from giving you their money up front. It could mean better prices for them in the future. It could mean having a special relationship with your company.

Since you don't yet have an established business, the way to do this is to make a deal with someone who already has a customer base that your product/service should appeal to. Yes, you'll have to split your profits with him—but it will get you up and running.

The great thing about customer financing is that the only debt you incur is the obligation to produce the product/service. And producing it puts you in business. You don't have to give up equity to investors. You don't need collateral for a loan. You don't have to worry at night because your nest egg is at risk.

Getting Yourself Up to Speed: Learning the Ropes While You Keep Your Day Job

I firmly believe that one of the best (possibly *the* best) ways to grow wealthy is to start your own business. And as a reluctant entrepreneur, you do it while still having the security of a regular salary. By keeping your day job, you have a chance to learn everything you need to know about running a business . . . without worrying about how you're going to pay the mortgage.

The fastest, easiest, and surest way to soak up all that knowledge is to get yourself a mentor—someone who's successfully done what you want to do.

This is hardly a new idea.

In the late Middle Ages and during the Renaissance, budding young artists learned their craft by being apprenticed to a master. Rembrandt did it. He learned from Pieter Lastman, one of the greatest artists of the seventeenth century. Michelangelo studied under Donatello, the greatest sculptor of his time. This system was responsible for many of the greatest artists and musicians in history.

Other skills—like masonry, carpentry, and boatbuilding—were also taught through apprenticeship programs. Today, it is still the primary method for training electricians, plumbers, and other tradesmen.

Traditionally, here's how the apprenticeship system works:

Stage 1: Novice

Being a novice is about learning the basics under the guidance of a master teacher. Not necessarily a master doer. It would be a waste of time to connect with someone who is a master at doing what you wanted to learn but incapable of teaching it to you.

Forget the old adage "Those who can, do; those who cannot, teach." Doing and teaching are two very different skills. At this stage of the game, you would want to connect with someone who is an expert at communicating the basics.

Stage 2: Journeyman

As a journeyman, you learn the things that most teachers cannot teach you. You discover the how-to secrets that are largely invisible to outsiders. This is when you move from understanding about a skill to becoming competent at actually practicing it.

The way to do that—to put a noble name on it—is through *mimesis*, the process of copying. In other words, you would copy those who have already mastered the skill. You would mimic what they do.

Stage 3: Master-in-Training

Only now—after putting in the time to learn the basics and develop some competence—would you be ready to connect with someone who practices your skill at a world-class level. Now you can take advantage of the opportunity to learn tricks and techniques you might not discover on your own for decades.

For reluctant entrepreneurs, the learning process isn't nearly as time-consuming. For one thing, you usually start with a basic understanding of the business you want to go into. And you can learn a lot more just by reading and doing your own research. But you can accelerate your progress by working with a mentor.

> *"Mentoring is a brain to pick, an ear to listen, and a push in the right direction."*
>
> —*John C. Crosby*

As a marketer, I had a mentor . . . a true master. I wouldn't be where I am today without JSN's mentorship. When he looked at me, he saw potential. He took the time to help me learn how to sell things and build businesses. Because of his mentorship, I was able to go from an income of $75,000 to one of more than $250,000 in 18 months. Then from $250,000 to more than a million dollars one year later. That's what a mentor can do for you.

HOW DO YOU FIND A MENTOR?

Look around your industry for successful businesspeople who retired two to five years ago. (During their first two years of retirement, they are still enjoying their extended vacation and haven't yet realized the tedium of playing golf all day. After five years, they may be a little too out of touch.) Make a list of five such individuals. Then write each one a nice letter telling him that you admire his accomplishments and hope he can give you some business advice.

If he lives nearby, offer to take him to lunch. If not, ask if he has time for a short phone call. Whether in person or over the phone, ask lots of questions. Listen attentively to his answers. With any luck, your personalities will click . . . and you'll have someone who will help you now and in the future.

A FEW EXAMPLES OF PEOPLE I'VE PERSONALLY MENTORED

- CF built her specialized physical therapy business from zero to $90,000 in 15 months.
- AS's nutritional-supplement business—just five years old—is grossing $5 million, netting more than 20 percent.
- JF's educational program for children is paying him close to $100,000 a year after less than three years.
- WC made $250,000 in less than 18 months—on top of his regular salary—by running a mail-order business on the side.
- PR built his health-product business to more than $20 million in six years (and became a multimillionaire in the process).
- KY's business pays her a very nice salary—plus she shares $500,000 in profits from a career-counseling program that's less than 10 years old.

PUTTING FEAR ON YOUR SIDE

Having your own business is not the only way to get rich, but it is the way that most people do it. Statistically speaking, it is your most likely road to success. It is the only way I know to generate serious cash flow in a relatively short period of time. It also gives you a chance to eventually become super-rich—to join the $50-million-plus club.

So accept the fact that you are cautious by nature. Be happy about that, because, as I said, your fear of taking risks and your instinctive desire for stability will work in your favor. But don't let that fear keep you from taking action.

By taking action, I mean doing what makes sense for the reluctant entrepreneur you are. (You're not going to even think about quitting your job until your business is up and running and profitable.)

Briefly, your strategy should include the following:

- Investigating time-management systems to find one that works for you.
- Understanding your options for financing your business.
- Getting someone to act as your mentor—a retired business owner who is willing to teach you what you need to know and encourage you to take the steps you have to take.
- Making a decision about exactly which business you want to start.
- If possible, getting a full- or part-time job in the industry you want to be in, ideally in the marketing department—then learning everything you can about how that business sells its products.
- Once you understand how the marketing works, preparing to test the waters yourself. Maybe on the Internet. Maybe by selling your products at flea markets or offering your services through related businesses.

- Reading *Ready, Fire, Aim,* my book on growing a business. That will give you the details of what you need to do to take your business from inception to $100 million in annual revenues and beyond.

You won't accomplish anything if you don't move forward. Even if your first step is a small one—like scheduling an informational interview with a bigwig in your industry—do something to get your new venture off the ground.

CHAPTER 5

THE MAGIC HAPPENS WHEN YOU HIRE SUPERSTARS

To run a successful business, top-notch marketing is critical. You can't do without it. High-quality products and services— definitely important. Good ideas—essential. But you can get all of these things, and more, if you have one thing.

I'm talking about the right people to help build, operate, and grow your business.

There are bad employees, mediocre employees, good employees, excellent employees, and superstars.

You must fire bad and mediocre employees quickly, give good employees a short window of time to become excellent, and treat your excellent employees well. I'll explain what I mean by that a little later in this chapter. But first, let's talk about superstars.

Superstars are dedicated and hardworking. They know their stuff. They understand and care about the business. But with their rare combination of intelligence and ambition, they can do something for you that you can't do on your own. They can—and will—take your business to new levels of success . . . if you let them.

One excellent employee is worth three good employees. But one superstar is priceless.

RECOGNIZING SUPERSTAR POTENTIAL

About 10 years ago, I got a call from one of my clients. "Jim," one of his junior copywriters—a young man I had recommended to him—was about to be fired.

I was surprised. I had spent some time with Jim and thought he had what it takes to eventually become a key person in my client's business. I saw him as a future superstar.

I asked my client what happened.

"He's hopeless," he told me. "We haven't been able to use any of the copy he's written for us. What's more, he's insolent. And cocky."

I admitted that the kid had a tendency to exaggerate his own importance, but I argued that he really did have a lot of natural talent.

"Let me work with him," I said.

I had put my reputation on the line. I didn't want to be proven wrong. And the moment I began working with Jim on his copy, I could see that he was as good as I remembered. He had an instinctive understanding of marketing. And within three months, he wrote a sales letter for my client that was the breakthrough of the year.

One success followed another. A year later, Jim had not only written a string of strong promotions, he had created several promising products. I told my client that he needed to make a new deal with Jim. I suggested that he let Jim start his own division and give him a significant share of the profits it would produce.

"If you don't," I said, "I'll hire him myself to start a business for me. And in two or three years, I guarantee it will be making millions."

My client grudgingly agreed. Today, he insists that he never had any negative feelings about Jim. He tells me my recollection of events is wrong.

In any case, Jim is now my client's most successful division head. He has built his sales from zero to more than $100 million . . . with no end in sight.

That is what a superstar can do for your business.

KNOWING WHAT YOU'RE LOOKING FOR

Most of the successful businesspeople I know rely on one or several superstars to help them grow and run their businesses. An entrepreneurial business that has only one superstar (you) can grow only to a certain degree. If you are typical, you can develop a healthy $10 million business by yourself. If you are extraordinary, you can do significantly better. (I know one entrepreneur who singlehandedly built an $80 million business.) But with the help of a superstar, you can do it much faster and easier.

Your superstar will learn your secrets faster than you can explain them. He'll take on any challenge. He'll figure out solutions before he tells you about problems. And he will share (or exceed) your enthusiasm and vision.

When I first wrote about this subject, I was working with three such superstars. Each was running a business with revenues of about $10 million. Today, those companies have increased their revenues to $50 million, $55 million, and $60 million. And it was done with very little help from me.

From the very beginning, you have to keep your eyes open for potential superstars. The likeliest candidates are people who are already working for you. Which means you should never settle for second best when filling any position.

Everyone you hire should have:

- **A strong sense of urgency.** All of your employees should understand that deadlines are made to be met and that speed is money. They should also understand that business is business . . . and it is serious.
- **A strong work ethic.** You want people who show up early and are ready to go . . . people who are on time for meetings and appointments. A pattern of showing up late for anything is a sign of not caring.
- **Respect for your customers.** Your customers invest their time and money with you. The primary mission of every one of your employees should be to serve them.

HOW DO YOU FIND THESE PEOPLE?

Think about what executive recruiters do. When they call Person A with a job opportunity and Person A is not interested, they end up with three phone numbers or e-mail addresses for people Person A knows.

So when you have a job opening, think about all the people you know, especially when you're looking to fill a middle- or upper-level position. If none of them are right for the job, call them anyway. They may know someone who is. Keep collecting names and numbers and making more phone calls.

If you are looking for more of an entry-level employee, try advertising in a trade publication. But do some research first. Read the ads the publication normally prints and make your ad better. Make your position sound rewarding and exciting. If there is room for advancement, mention it.

You can also use Career Builder, Monster, eHire, and other online job search engines. You'll probably have to sift through hundreds of applications, 99 percent of them useless. But you may luck out.

Even better than advertisements . . . and far better than online job search engines . . . is networking. I look for possible employees everywhere I go.

When I attend industry events (which I often do), the cocktail parties are my favorite networking places. (You get a real feel for the personality and style of the people you meet.) When I give presentations, I tell my audience that I am available to talk about job opportunities. When my kids were younger, I'd talk to other parents while attending their soccer games.

You can network *anywhere*. Wherever there are people, there's a chance to find someone who might be a good fit for your company.

When you meet a potential superstar, start a relationship. Strike up a conversation. Find out as much as you can about him. Show interest. Follow his career. Offer to help. When the time is right, drop hints. "If you ever want to do such and such . . . give me a call." Say it every time you see him. The message will get through. Eventually, he will call.

When he does, hire him. Work with him closely for several months until you've seen what he can do. If he has the potential you're looking for, it will be apparent. Invite him to share your future. Give him a place on your core team.

Superstars are rare birds. If they don't know their worth when you hire them, they will soon enough. It's much smarter (and cheaper in the long run) to treat them like partners-in-training from the get-go.

I recognized one young man's potential in the late 1990s. At the time, he was making about $36,000. I convinced one of my clients to hire him. And within a year, he had devised and launched a new product that was more successful than any my client had seen in years. We immediately raised his compensation and gave him a sizeable share of the profits. Today, he generates more than $60 million in sales for my client. He makes a seven-figure income. He's worth every penny of it and more.

I recommended another outstanding young man to a different client. This time, the client refused to put him on a partnership path. Why, I cannot say. At any rate, after two years of doing great work and feeling unappreciated, the young man quit and went into business on his own. He is now one of my client's major competitors. He has sales of more than $30 million and has hired some of my client's good people away from him.

It doesn't matter where you are in your business-building process—even if you're still in the learning phase—you need to start thinking about hiring superstars.

Keep in mind that superstars are few and far between. Don't let scarcity tempt you to accept less than the best. You cannot make an ordinary person extraordinary. It will eat up all your time and end in failure.

Start your search now. Go to industry functions. Talk to people. Even if you can't yet afford another salary, start looking.

> *"Hire people who are better than you are, then leave them to get on with it. . . . Look for people who will aim for the remarkable, who will not settle for the routine."*
>
> —*David Ogilvy*

THE CARE AND FEEDING OF A SUPERSTAR

Let your superstars know why you think they're special. Don't flatter them. Just tell them the truth. Tell them that you want them to rise all the way to the top. Spend time with them, quality time. Teach them everything you know. Don't hold back anything. And, very important, give them room to grow. Superstars die in bureaucratic environments.

Specifically, here's how to keep your superstars motivated:

- Without being foolhardy, give them authority. Achievement-oriented people enjoy freedom, power, prestige, and a good challenge. Give them enough rope to hang themselves but not so much that they can hang you too.
- Give them feedback. Mix the positive and the negative. Praise your good people, yes. Praise them, publicly and sincerely, when it's appropriate. But don't be afraid to criticize them—privately—when it is warranted. The best employees don't need to be coddled, manipulated, or managed. They need mentoring and they need a challenge. They will accept criticism so long as it is fair.
- Give them advice. Great people will teach themselves most of the technical parts of your business. They will also figure out much of the left-brain stuff if you give them the freedom and resources to find the answers. What they can't do themselves is learn the inside secrets of your business. These are the vital but invisible tricks of the trade that you have discovered the hard way. Don't make your protégés learn these secrets on their own. Teach them yourself. That will speed up their success, which will speed up your rewards.
- Give your best people good work to do and a lot of it. The ultimate reward for superstars is the pleasure they get from doing a good job. Make their work interesting, complex, and difficult—and they will stick with you.
- Money is not the biggest motivator for superstars, but it can't be ignored. Pay your superstars at least 10 percent more than market, but don't overpay them thinking that doing so will keep them loyal. You must compensate superstars well—and always before they ask. Their compensation must be a bit larger than they could get elsewhere. If you're stingy, you risk losing them.

The fundamental principle governing your relationship with your employees is goodwill. If you care about your superstars and want them to succeed, they will stay with you. If you see them simply as human energy to fuel your own engine, they will eventually leave you.

Remember that along with their many other positive qualities, exceptional employees are usually very perceptive. They will know if you are faking. They will understand that they are better off working with someone who wants them to succeed than with someone who wants them to help build his own career.

One way to make it clear that you value their contribution is to schedule time—at least once a year—to talk to them about the work they're doing. Take each one out for a nice lunch and, while you're enjoying the meal, ask questions like these:

"What do you like best about your job?"
"What do you like least?"
"Which of your recent accomplishments are you most proud of?"
"What is the most important thing you have learned this year?"
"Other than yourself, who do you think is our most valuable employee?"
"What three things would you like to do more of? Less of?"
"How can I make your job more rewarding?"

Your goal is twofold: to find out if they are experiencing any problems, and to see if they have any ideas that will help you make your business better.

"When we treat man as he is, we make him worse than he is; when we treat him as if he already were what he potentially could be, we make him what he should be."
—*Johann Wolfgang von Goethe*

HOW TO STRUCTURE A SUPERSTAR ORGANIZATION

You should have superstars in every facet of your business. When your future is at stake, there is no room for mediocrity.

Identify the key functions you need to meet your business goals. Then, when considering people to fill each of those roles, ask yourself honestly, "Is he really great?" If he's not, look for someone else.

Having six people reporting to you is ideal. If you have fewer than that, your business won't be able to grow as fast as you might like. If you have more, you won't be able to keep track of what everyone is doing.

Having a six-superstar business is a wonderful thing. It will make your business six times stronger right away. But you can double that by insisting that every one of your superstars hires at least one superstar himself. And you will increase the growth potential of your business by 3,600 percent when all six of your superstars have six superstars working for them.

Some superstars don't need to be told to hire superstars. Some do. Don't leave this all-important task to chance.

If top-notch talent is limited to a single level—the one directly below you—your business will never reach its potential. New projects and possibilities will either fail or be put off indefinitely because your best people won't be able to handle them.

When Michael Bloomberg was elected mayor of New York City he insisted that all top city managers have a "replacement" for themselves in their employ. I don't like that way of putting it—it's too negative. But the idea of having a superstar in your corner to take over your current responsibilities so you can move up and on to greater opportunities . . . that, I like.

Your initial six-superstar business might consist of the following:

- Financial accounting superstar
- Marketing superstar
- Copywriting superstar
- Sales superstar
- Operations superstar
- IT superstar

Then, when all six of your superstars have hired their own superstar-in-training, your 12-superstar business would look like this:

- Your financial accounting superstar + his bookkeeping superstar
- Your marketing superstar + his assistant marketing superstar
- Your copywriting superstar + his junior copywriting superstar
- Your sales superstar + his assistant sales superstar
- Your operations superstar + his assistant operations superstar
- Your IT superstar + his computer tech superstar

Before long:

- Your financial accounting superstar will have become your superstar CFO.
- Your marketing superstar will have become your superstar VP of Marketing.
- Your copywriting superstar will have become your head copywriter and associate publisher.

- Your sales superstar will have become your head of sales.
- Your operations superstar will have become your COO.
- Your IT superstar will have become your VP of Technology and Telecommunications.

That's a company *full* of superstar employees all working toward one goal: the success of your business.

I was a superstar for one of my first mentors. Through his careful tutoring, we were able to take a startup marketing business and grow it to $65 million in about seven years. His son took on my former role and helped us double that business in three years.

After we sold the business, I partnered with a brilliant businessman who saw in me a marketing superstar who could grow his business. And it did grow—from $8 million to $26 million in one year.

We then located six more truly gifted superstars. They helped us (they did more than help) grow the business from $26 million to $260 million.

> *"Start with good people, lay out the rules, communicate with your employees, motivate them and reward them. If you do all those things effectively, you can't miss."*
>
> —Lee Iacocca

THE BEST INVESTMENT YOU WILL EVER MAKE

I was once asked, "What's the best investment you ever made?"

My answer? Undeniably, it was the time and money I invested in great people. Let me give you some examples:

- SR—an ex-con I mentored in 1980. He ran two multi-million-dollar businesses for a business partner and then became my partner in two more. My investment in SR has returned at least $5 million.

- MW—a former drug addict and a childhood friend. I worked with MW in the early 1990s. He became a very successful copywriter and then my partner. Return to date: more than $1 million.
- JK—Fresh out of college, JK was the boyfriend of our children's babysitter when I began teaching him about entrepreneurship. Today, I am his partner in three successful small businesses. I do nothing more than have lunch with him once a month. And every time, he hands me a check for at least $10,000.
- DH—a doctor with a family practice when I met him in the mid 1990s. I began working with him three years ago in return for a small percentage of his side-business revenues. Like JK, I meet DH once a month and he hands me a check. Every month, that check has been getting bigger. Last month, it was $17,142.
- RS—Fresh out of a job when I hired her in the late 1990s, RS developed an $8 million business that gives me a $200,000+ dividend every year.
- LP—a "problem" employee about to be fired when I started working with him. Today, he's in charge of a $60 million division of a company I have an interest in. Last year, his division produced more than $20 million in profits!

When you invest in great people, the return compounds. Great people—well-taught and motivated—hire, train, and motivate other great people. And that expands your business and your wealth geometrically.

Investing in great people can not only make you rich, it will simplify your life. In the early stages, you'll spend a significant amount of time on your protégés and get little back. But then they become independent and operate on your behalf without needing much (if anything) from you. And even if they strike out on their own, they will always be happy to help you out.

More than half of the wealth I have came from people I believed in. Put differently: If I had spent my career trying only to make myself rich instead of helping to develop the careers of others, I'd be a much poorer person today.

CHAPTER 6

MASTERING THE ART OF BUSINESS RELATIONSHIPS

In thinking back on my professional life, I can recall relationships that—however beneficial they may have seemed at the outset—eventually turned into sticky, swampy problems. Had I asked myself before getting involved with any of these people "Is this someone who sees the world of business the way I do?" I might have avoided a good deal of stress. In some cases, I might have saved a bundle of money.

The fact is, who you associate with is extremely important—in your business and your personal life. As a general rule, you become like the people you spend the most time with. This is an especially important consideration in business, where we come into contact with all sorts of individuals—brilliant and motivated, brilliant but lazy, dull but dedicated, dull and lazy.

You want to develop relationships with the smart, the hardworking, and the well-connected. You want to deal with people who are relatively trustworthy and honest. (I say "relatively" because I believe only the phoniest and scariest of people pretend to be 100 percent pure in these virtues.) And you want to work with people who have the same basic idea you have about what is good and true in life. It also makes sense to search out people who have strengths that complement your own.

Does that mean you should never spend time with "friends in low places"? Of course not.

Two short blocks from my office, just across the railroad tracks, sits O'Connor's Pub. It's an unassuming place, a neighborhood hangout with an above-average percentage of blue-collar bullshit artists, drifters, and lovable losers.

I certainly don't want to become an oddball like T-Bone, the ex-con car mechanic, or Crazy Dave. But, frankly, I enjoy their company. And sometimes, when I'm at a swanky affair, surrounded by wealthy and powerful people, I find myself wondering what the boys at O'Connor's are up to.

I have a wide array of friendships. And I'm not going to give any of them up. I don't suggest you give yours up either. At this point in my life, I am what I am—and the people I associate with aren't going to change me.

But when you're just starting out in business, you are easily influenced. So it pays to think about the other guy's character when you're considering forming a new relationship.

THE INTANGIBLE REWARDS OF ESTABLISHING BUSINESS RELATIONSHIPS WITH THE RIGHT PEOPLE

Choosing great people to work with will hugely accelerate the speed at which you achieve success. But that is just one of the rewards you will enjoy. Surrounding yourself with great people means:

- Having more fun coming up with breakthrough business ideas—because the ideas you get by thinking with others tend to be better than those you get on your own.
- Enjoying your successes more—because you have good people to share them with.
- Feeling good about yourself—when you see everyone around you learning and progressing.

THE RELUCTANT ENTREPRENEUR'S GUIDE TO MAKING FRIENDS IN HIGH PLACES

If you could be on a first-name basis with anyone in your trade or your industry, who would it be? Whose power or position would you most like to gain access to? Who among all the people you know of could have the most positive impact on your future?

Imagine what it would be like to have an address book full of people like this—people you could turn to for help or advice whenever you need it.

Well, the time has come to start building that network.

A publisher whose career has been (to use a useful cliché) meteoric told me she reads the trade journals. And when she sees a story bylined by a powerful person she'd like to have in her network, she writes a personal note complimenting him on his article.

"It's amazing how often you'll get a reply," she notes. "And how open they are to starting a correspondence."

What better way is there to start relationships with experts in your field than by complimenting them on their industry knowledge?

Here's how you do it . . .

Make a list of all the people who could give your career a real boost. Your list could include people who run successful businesses similar to yours. It could also include people in completely unrelated fields who have qualities or skills you'd like to have yourself.

Start with the person at the top of your list. Think about something he has done that you admire. It might be a product he recently developed. It might be the standard of customer service he set for his business. It might be something he has written or accomplished or an award he has won. Anything you genuinely admire.

On some very nice, dignified stationery, you're going to write him a handwritten note expressing your feelings.

Don't fawn. Be direct.

End with some sort of effort to establish contact. You might ask his opinion on a certain matter, suggest a possible joint venture, or simply request a personal interview. You can, for example, say something like this: "I know you are a very busy man—but if you ever have a spare half-hour, I'd love the chance to get some advice from you on my own business."

Don't expect to get an answer to every note you write, but do expect to get some responses. If you commit yourself to this program, you will eventually be on a first-name basis with a handful of very influential people. This will have a positive—though unpredictable—impact on your future.

TRADE SHOWS: THE QUICKEST, EASIEST WAY TO MAKE CAREER-BUILDING CONTACTS

I tend to shy away from industry events. But every time I force myself to attend one, I am rewarded. A trip several years ago to a trade show in the health industry resulted in a multimillion-dollar deal with a publisher I literally bumped into on the exhibition floor. A cocktail party at a trade show in New Orleans led to a relationship that completely revolutionized the way I thought about a certain type of business.

If you have ever attended one of these functions, you know what I mean. Unless you wear a paper bag over your head, you can't help but make some useful contacts.

So do something right now. Take a look at a trade publication for your industry. Check out the calendar of upcoming events. Pick one that offers you the best chance to meet as many people as possible. Book yourself an airline ticket and make time in your schedule.

12 WAYS TO GET PEOPLE TO WANT TO DO BUSINESS WITH YOU

I like to think of myself as an amiable guy, but I wouldn't claim to be charismatic. Charismatic is an adjective I would apply to someone like Jay Leno or Tony Robbins. Bill Clinton is supposed to be very charismatic. I know die-hard conservatives who changed their views about him after speaking to him for just five minutes.

Wouldn't it be great to have that kind of effect on people? Wouldn't it feel good to know that you have the ability to make everyone you meet like you . . . and want to work with you?

Just a few hours ago, such a man came to my office. He had just taken over managing my bond account after my longtime account manager retired. I didn't want to like this young upstart because I resented it when my old account manager left. I felt (irrationally) abandoned. But within five minutes, we were talking about cigars and martial arts. By the time he left a half-hour later (we were scheduled to meet for only 15 minutes), I had promised him more of my business. I had also given him a copy of my latest book and a $20 cigar!

He should have given me a cigar. But that's the power of charisma.

Many salespeople are charismatic. You meet them. You like them. You buy from them. Even when they don't have the best product or the best pricing.

Charismatic people seem to be born that way. They have an uncanny, natural ability to sell almost anything, including their ideas. They don't follow the usual rules. They smile a lot. They chat a lot.

Do they have skills that the rest of us—the non-gifted lot—can learn?

Absolutely!

Here are 12 ways you can become more charismatic and get more out of all your business relationships. Most of them are based on principles identified by Robert Cialdini in his book *Influence: The Psychology of Persuasion*:

1. People tend to do business with people they like. So behave in a way that makes you likable. Be polite and patient. Avoid being crude, rude, gruff, or impatient.
2. People are attracted to people who keep their word. That means when you make a promise, do exactly what you promised. Do it by the deadline you promised—or sooner.
3. People trust people who have their best interests at heart. They will think you have their best interests at heart when you give them advice that benefits them more than it benefits you.
4. People want to do business with people who are experts in their fields. So first you need to actually become an expert in your field through practice, research, training, education, and study. Then you need to do things (such as writing articles and books or giving speeches) that demonstrate your expertise to potential customers and business associates.
5. People feel comfortable giving money to people who are honest, ethical, and aboveboard. So don't lie in your marketing materials (or elsewhere). Telling the truth is much more effective.
6. People are attracted to people who are physically attractive, or at least not physically repulsive. So eat right. Exercise. Stay fit. Be well-groomed. Dress well. And pay attention to your personal hygiene.
7. People feel better with people who seem to be "real." The best way to show that you're a regular guy is to be cordial, friendly, and genuinely interested in others.

Instead of talking about yourself, ask about them. Ask about their company, their job, their industry, even their family and hobbies.

8. People respond to people who listen and pay attention to what they are saying. Remember the old cliché: You have two ears and one mouth, because you should listen twice as much as you talk.

9. People feel comfortable with people who are like them. The trick here is to identify one thing you have in common with the other person. It could be golf, kids, pets, or anything else. Then use that to cement a bond between you.

10. People are attracted to people who are humble. So don't be a braggart. And never discuss how much money you make.

11. People are impressed by people who seem busy. That's why you should never tell a prospective customer that things are slow and you really need his business. Think about doctors. How would you feel if you walked into a doctor's office and you were the only patient? Wouldn't you wonder how good he was? As much as you hate it when you have to sit there and wait, don't you feel more assured when a doctor's waiting room is packed? Of course you do.

12. People want to be surrounded by helpful people—people who make their lives easier and save them time. They also prefer to deal with people who are flexible and accommodating, not rigid and difficult.

Which of these people-pleasing skills do you have already? Congratulate yourself for acquiring them, and practice them more.

Which ones do you still need to develop? You can't do it overnight, but you can—and should—work on them over time.

A SIMPLE TRICK THAT WILL MAKE IMPORTANT PEOPLE WANT TO TALK TO YOU

There are two ways to instantly make a good impression on just about anyone. Flattery works. So does asking questions about something they know a lot about.

Case in point . . .

The other day, I was sitting in my office working on some disagreeable problem when the door cracked open and the head of a man I'd never seen before popped through. My first reaction was alarm and annoyance. Then he gave me a big smile, and I felt compelled to smile back.

"I've come to ask you a question," he said, and stepped inside.

I suspected he was up to something but I couldn't resist. "What is that?" I responded.

He said that he had heard I was a marketing genius and was hoping I could give him some quick advice on a marketing decision he was trying to make.

"I'm kind of busy right now," I said.

"A minute of your time is all I'm asking," he replied. He looked at his watch and added, "I'll time it."

How could I say no?

"Go ahead," I consented. "Ask your question."

He sat down. "How does a person know if he has any talent for marketing?" he asked.

It was, in retrospect, a devilishly clever question. On the one hand, it was too big to answer in an hour, let alone a minute. On the other hand, it was indirectly flattering (the assumption that I would know), and so I was seduced into carrying on.

We ended up spending an hour together, at the end of which he left with:

- a list of three potential employers he could contact
- specific recommendations for improving his marketing skills
- the right to address me by my first name

Not a bad accomplishment for someone I normally wouldn't have given the time of day.

You can put this powerful technique to work in person, by phone, by e-mail, or by mail. But whatever means of communication you choose, do it with a smile. A smile lets your target know that you like him and mean him well. A smile buys you enough time to ask the question. If the question is the right one, the rest will be easy.

(You convey a smile on the phone by smiling when you speak. You smile in writing by using a simple, cheerful opening sentence and ending it with an exclamation point.)

So, here's what you do:

- Make a list of six people you'd like to get to know. They could be potential partners or mentors or the protégés or associates of people in high places.
- Go to speak with them personally, phone them, e-mail them, or write them.
- Remember to lead with a smiling salutation.
- Then ask a question that allows them to talk about something they know.

Make this a habit.

HOW TO GET OTHERS TO TELL YOU THEIR MOST VALUABLE SUCCESS SECRETS— A TECHNIQUE I LEARNED FROM A SELF-MADE MULTIMILLIONAIRE

Ted Nicholas, the advertising guru and self-made multimillionaire, leads an enviable life. Married to a beautiful, intelligent woman, he lives in Switzerland and Florida, travels extensively, plays top-level tennis, and works when he wants and as much as he wants.

Last time he was in South Florida for business, we met to catch up. The conversation started with chit-chat—how's the family, nice weather, what about those Yankees, and so on. But that didn't last long. Ted wanted to know about me. What was I doing? What new projects was I involved in? What new marketing tests had I observed?

I told Ted how all my business interests were doing. I told him about my new projects, even revealed to him my theories about which are going to work very well and why.

"This is information I shouldn't be telling him," I thought to myself. Yet I kept talking. I told him I was looking at investing in a list-management company in New York. I even told him where it was located. I told him about a hush-hush public offering I was marginally involved with.

It occurred to me that this was one of Ted's success secrets. He got all kinds of good stuff from me—and I promised myself that his was a conversational trick I'd practice more often.

If you are lucky enough to be in the company of a successful businessman, don't waste your precious time talking about baseball . . . or, worse, yourself. Take advantage of the situation and ask a few questions. Questions as simple as these . . .

- What was your biggest business challenge this year?
- What is the accomplishment you are most proud of?
- Have you met any interesting people?

Here's what will happen if you do:

First, you will be surprised at how forthcoming your conversation partner is.

Second, you will be astonished by how much you learn. People will tell you the most amazing things—sometimes even their most valuable secrets—if you let them.

"Small opportunities are often the beginning of great enterprises."
—*Demosthenes*

NEVER PASS UP THE OPPORTUNITY TO MAKE A CONNECTION THAT CAN DO YOU SOME GOOD

Some years ago, I saw a play titled *Six Degrees of Separation*. It explored the idea that any two people are connected by no more than five other people. You know someone . . . who knows someone . . . who knows someone . . . and you never know where this might lead. So whenever you meet someone, take the time to explore the potential of that relationship.

I was reminded of the value of this on a business trip years ago. A friend and I were on our way back to the States after visiting a development project we're involved with in Nicaragua.

While waiting for our flight, my friend struck up a conversation with three scruffy-looking men. These were not the sort of guys I'd expect us to have anything in common with. But they turned out to be two 40-something surfers and their dad. They were in Nicaragua to surf and to look at some property one of them had purchased that was about an hour's drive from our development.

We swapped Nicaragua stories for a while. Then my friend told them about our development. They'd heard of it. They had read about it in an article published in *Surf Express* magazine. One of them said he wanted to talk to us about opening a restaurant on our property. (He was already a restaurant owner in Tampa.) He was also interested in helping us develop a marina. (He owned one of those too.)

Who would have thought?

And this potentially lucrative connection was entirely due to my friend, who ignored their crumpled clothes and bearded faces and started a conversation.

MAKE EVERY PERSONAL ENCOUNTER COUNT

According to Nicholas Boothman, author of *How to Make People Like You*, what you do in the first few minutes of every personal encounter determines how people will respond to you later on. First impressions do count, Boothman believes, more than most people realize.

And it's not just the very first impression. It's the first impression you give each and every time you greet someone.

So do the following:

- Make eye contact. Always look the other person directly in the eye, if only for a moment.
- Be the first to smile. Let your smile, as well as your body language, show that you're happy to see him.
- Make your "Hi!" or "Hello!" sound friendly.
- Take the lead. Extend your hand first.
- Shake his hand strongly. Shake it like you mean it.
- Lean toward him. An almost imperceptible forward tilt will subtly indicate your interest in and openness to the other person.

Here's an extra tip: However much you can, know what you want out of every new relationship or new encounter before you begin it. This will help you channel that positive first impression into something meaningful.

SEEK OUT MUTUALLY-BENEFICIAL PARTNERSHIPS

Every ambitious entrepreneur should be open to partnership deals, including marketing joint ventures. But you have to be selective.

In my view, the ideal partner has the following characteristics:

- He has something besides money to offer the partnership that you don't. This might be intelligence, assertiveness, creativity, perspicacity, a capacity for networking, or an indomitable spirit.
- He is long-term-oriented. He understands that building a business takes time.
- He is fair-minded.
- He is loyal.

Of those, the last two are absolutely essential.

Let me tell you why I see it that way.

I have been in many successful partnerships. The best of these were with men and women who had all the qualities listed here and more. But some of them have been with people who had nothing valuable to contribute except the willingness to give it a try. I can think of two right off the bat that netted hundreds of thousands of dollars. I was happy to give those partners their share, and I think I was right in feeling that way.

Partnerships often deconstruct because of arguments over who does what. Or over how much money each partner is making. I think the reason I've had such good experiences with mine has to do with three things, all attitude related:

1. I recognize that however much I bring to the table, it's not enough.
2. I know from experience that everyone, every partner, has something to teach me.
3. I know I'm a better performer and can make tougher decisions when I have a partner to run ideas by.

More importantly, I have a special—and I think correct—view of how value in a business should be decided. The way I see it, the value of each partner's shares are decided at the outset, based on the resources (intellectual, capital, reputation, etc.) each is contributing. All contributions made later—even if one partner ends up running the business while the other partner simply attends meetings now and then—should be paid for on an arms-length, free-market basis.

If you do it that way, you will never have any need to fight about who does what. If one partner wants to stop working, no problem. Just cut his salary (for working) and use it to hire his replacement. If your arms-length evaluations for such contributions are accurate, you'll have just enough money to pay for a very good person.

Here's another thing. Some partnerships begin with one partner contributing most of the valuable work and end up with the other partner taking the lead. If you bicker in the first instance, you'll end up screaming later on.

LK, a colleague, once said, "Never begin a venture as a partnership unless you're convinced your partner brings something irreplaceable to the table. If that's not the case, one of two things will happen. You'll fail and blame each other, or succeed and fight over it."

I'd say this to LK: If I had applied your standard to all of the partnerships I've been in, I would have been in very few indeed. And I can count up millions of dollars' worth of income I'd have given up.

Don't be afraid of partnerships. Pick partners you trust and make sure you agree on how these sorts of things should be fairly worked out. Ask a few "What if . . . ?" questions before you sign the contract. Then get down to business and enjoy working with each other.

IT DOESN'T TAKE MUCH TO MAINTAIN RELATIONSHIPS WITH ALL YOUR IMPORTANT CONTACTS—EVEN HUNDREDS OF THEM

Your power network is comprised of all the people you know who can make a positive difference in your future. They include your mentors, consultants, competitors, vendors, colleagues, and people in high places who have resources and connections you lack.

Is there a limit to the number of people you should have in your power network?

No. You should have as many as can be of benefit to you. These are the people you can call on pretty much whenever you need to. With that as the criterion, the number can be large.

Can you maintain so many relationships? I think so.

Since most successful people are busy with their own lives, they don't require a lot of your time. It's enough for them to hear from you now and then. Even once a year will do. Just make it something positive or pleasing.

If you write one personal note or e-mail per day (as I do), you can easily keep in touch with more than 300 members of your power network.

It will take only a few minutes, and will be well worth it.

CHAPTER 7

HOW TO BECOME A MARKETING GENIUS

Years ago, I bought into a thriving art gallery. It was the fulfill-ment of a dream. When I fantasized about owning my own gallery (as I often did), I saw myself sitting in a comfortable leather chair, reading books about art. I imagined having con-versations with worldly people about art.

The reality was quite different.

The first thing my partner had me do was invite everyone I knew to come to our grand opening. I was excited. I couldn't wait to show the place off. But then he said, "As soon as we get them in the door, we'll get to work on them."

Huh? I didn't like the sound of that.

When the big day arrived, I dutifully followed him around and watched him "get to work" on our invited guests. I was ashamed and disappointed. I realized that the dream business I'd bought into wasn't really about the art. It was, in fact, based on hard-core selling.

I was embarrassed. I shouldn't have been so naïve. After all, I'd been in business for years. I should have known that the reason my partner had been so successful with this gallery was because he was an expert at *selling* art. He knew how to get people to come into the gallery, get them to buy, and then get them to buy again and again.

EVERY BUSINESS IS ABOUT THE SELLING

Every commercial enterprise—every restaurant, law office, hospital, building supplier, hardware store, and entertainment complex—survives and prospers as a result of its ability to attract customers and sell to them. Of all the skills you can develop, none is more basic to your success as an entrepreneur than learning how to do that well.

Corporate execs and even some CEOs can get away with not knowing marketing in a deep way. But that is not true for the inexperienced entrepreneur. You have no choice. You don't have the money to hire a professional team to do it for you.

You must start from scratch. You must build your business gradually by constantly asking yourself "How can I bring in new customers cost-efficiently?" and "How can I keep those customers buying?"

The answers to those questions make up what we call your Optimum Selling Strategy.

Your Optimum Selling Strategy is a combination of the advertising media you choose, your promotional copy, and your front-end and back-end offers.

What you're looking for is an approach that will have the greatest long-term benefit. Usually, that means finding the greatest number of high-value customers. That is, people who will buy your main, front-end product . . . and can then be converted to buyers of your back-end products for years into the future.

This chapter will take you through the fundamentals.

"The purpose of business is to create and keep a customer."
—Peter F. Drucker

THE BEAUTY OF DIRECT MARKETING

If you were in charge of marketing for a company like Coca Cola or American Express or Sony, you could spend millions on advertising. But you're not. So for you, direct marketing is the only way to go.

Through direct marketing, you evoke a direct response from your prospective customer. That response can be anything from making a purchase to returning a free-trial postcard to making a phone call to providing information on your web site.

You can do direct marketing on the Internet. You can also do it on radio, on television, with magazine and newspaper ads, and with sales letters sent through the mail.

What makes it ideal for the reluctant entrepreneur is that it allows you to:

- Inexpensively test different media, products, copy, and offers.
- Accurately measure the results.
- Quickly determine what works and what doesn't.

Here's how one of my clients took advantage of direct marketing on the Internet to discover their Optimum Selling Strategy . . .

The client sells information products. Of the many ways they tested to bring in new buyers and then convert them to long-term customers, two proved to be extremely effective:

1. Selling informational reports on other people's web sites. Then giving buyers a free subscription to their own daily e-zine—which sells those buyers all sorts of increasingly expensive back-end products.
2. Targeting search engine users with pay-per-click (PPC) ads offering a free special report. Then giving those who responded to the offer a free subscription to their e-zine with its back-end selling.

By tracking their back-end sales, my client found that those who had purchased the informational reports were worth considerably more over the long-term than those who had responded to the free-report offers.

So the next thing they tested was three levels of pricing for the informational reports: $20, $50, and $100. By tracking the spending habits of people who purchased the reports, they found that the $20 spenders were each worth about $6 extra per year. Those who spent $50 were worth about $50 extra per year. Interestingly, the ones who spent $100 were no more valuable, in terms of back-end buying, than those who spent $50.

Right now, in this market, my client's primary strategy for attracting the kind of customers they are looking for is to create and market as many $50 information reports as they can on the Internet. But just because this kind of offer has worked in the past doesn't mean it will always be the best offer. Markets change because culture does. Some of the fundamental psychological principles remain the same, but the individual elements of any marketing campaign will change over time.

So they test different price points, payment terms, and guarantees on a regular basis. They also test their promotional copy. They test headlines. They test leads. They test hard approaches against soft approaches, benefit-oriented pitches against idea-oriented ones. They test just about anything, so long as they think the element they are testing has a reasonable chance of increasing their response rate by a substantial margin.

The best source I know of for learning exactly how to do this is American Writers & Artists Inc. (AWAI). AWAI is the world's leading publisher of home-study programs for direct-response marketing. They can also teach you how to write killer promotional copy. The kind of copy that will motivate your prospects to respond to your offers.

For more information, go to http://www.awaionline.com/.

Meanwhile, let's take a look at the psychology behind the best marketing efforts. Because, ultimately, all marketing is a matter of persuading people to buy what you're selling.

MASTERING THE ART OF PERSUASION

Among the thousands of books that have been written about marketing, there are a dozen that every entrepreneur should have in his library. Among them are the classics:

* *Scientific Advertising* by Claude Hopkins
* *Ogilvy on Advertising* by David Ogilvy
* *Tested Advertising Methods* by John Caples and Fred E. Hahn
* *How to Make Your Advertising Make Money* by John Caples
* *Breakthrough Advertising* by Eugene M. Schwartz

To those I would add *Changing the Channel*, the book I co-wrote with MaryEllen Tribby.

And at the top of my list is a book written by an academic, a guy who had no experience as a marketer. In fact, he didn't even like marketers. His goal was to help consumers understand and resist the efforts of the marketing pros.

The book is *Influence: The Psychology of Persuasion* by Robert Cialdini. It never achieved great popularity among consumers. But some savvy marketers found that Cialdini's insights were very helpful for them. They started spreading the word. And before long, the book was a big hit with the very people Cialdini was doing battle with.

Influence became a business bestseller in 1984. Several updated editions followed, and the book continues to sell well. Cialdini has also become a much-admired speaker on marketing. In 2008, he published *Yes! 50 Scientifically Proven Ways to Be Persuasive* with co-authors Noah J. Goldstein and Steve J. Martin. This book expands on *Influence* in many ways. It presents a number of counterintuitive techniques for persuading people to act the way you want them to.

The action you want people to take, of course, is to buy your product. Cialdini's books—along with all the other books mentioned here—will help you make that happen.

But there's one secret in particular that I want to share with you now. It's something I learned by testing thousands and thousands of approaches. It starts with recognizing that your customers don't really *need* your product. So to motivate them to buy it, you have to make them *want* it.

That means understanding:

- The difference between wants and needs
- The difference between features and benefits
- The difference between benefits and deeper benefits

WHAT YOUR CUSTOMERS REALLY CARE ABOUT

When creating a sales promotion, don't make the mistake of making it about you. The customer wants to know what your product is going to do for him.

"In the selling arena," Jeffrey J. Fox advises in *How to Become a Rainmaker*, "customers don't care if you have a mortgage to pay . . . or if you need their business to win a contest . . . or why your shipments are late . . . or what you're like, where you went to school, or what sports you play."

He's right. Most of the time, most people care about themselves. So if you want potential customers to listen to what you have to say, make sure it appears as if you are talking about their favorite subject: them.

In other words, use the word "you" a lot more than you use the word "I."

THE DIFFERENCE BETWEEN WANTS AND NEEDS

In today's consumer-driven economy, it's easy to mistake a want for a need. Take a look at the following statements:

- "Sally needs a new wardrobe. The clothes she's wearing make her look silly."
- "John hates the way his hair looks. He says he needs a better barber."
- "I simply have to have that new handbag!"
- "We need a bigger house."
- "We need a nicer car."

None of those things are needs. They are not things you can't live without. Our actual needs are few. Air, water, food, shelter, transportation (sometimes), and some basic articles of clothing. Everything else we buy is based on wants.

Even when we buy things we need, our decisions are usually based on wants. We want a certain type of bread, a specific brand or style of clothes, a house in a particular neighborhood, and so on.

So if your customers don't need your product, how do you make them want it?

- In your promotional copy, you promise your prospective customer that taking a certain action (buying your product) will result in the satisfaction of a desire (want).
- You create a picture in your prospect's mind of the way he will feel when that desire is satisfied.
- You make specific claims about the benefits of your product, and then you prove those claims.
- You equate the feeling your prospect desires (the satisfaction of a want) with the purchase of your product.

Whether you find your customers through television or radio, magazines or newspapers, at home reading their mail or on the Internet, the formula is the same. The moment you forget that you are selling to wants rather than needs, your marketing efforts will falter.

THE DIFFERENCE BETWEEN FEATURES AND BENEFITS

To stimulate your prospect's desire for your product, you have to understand the difference between its features and its benefits. The example of a No. 2 pencil is often used to illustrate this. Here's how it's done . . .

A pencil has certain features:

- It is made of wood.
- It has a specific diameter.
- It contains a lead-composite filler of a certain type.
- It usually has an eraser at the end.

These features describe the objective qualities of the pencil. And if buying were an entirely rational process, selling it would simply be a matter of identifying those features.

But most purchases are made for emotional, not rational, reasons. Which means that you must convert the features of your product into benefits. For example, the features of a No. 2 pencil might be converted into the following benefits:

- Easy to sharpen.
- Comfortable to hold.
- Creates an impressive line.
- Makes correcting easy.

It's the benefits that you focus on in your copy.

(By the way, I once conducted a workshop on the difference between features and benefits using a No. 2 pencil that resulted in the identification of more than 100 benefits!)

THE DIFFERENCE BETWEEN BENEFITS AND DEEPER BENEFITS

Marketing geniuses take this one step further and identify the product's deeper benefits.

In our example, the marketing genius wouldn't be satisfied with the ordinary benefit of "easy to sharpen." He would ask himself, "Who is my target customer? And why might he want sharpening pencils to be easy?"

There's no single answer to such questions. It depends partly on who the target customer is. If he's an executive, his deeper reasons are going to be different from those of a college student.

Perhaps the executive wants more ease because he's buried in minutia. Perhaps he senses that if he could just get a little more spare time in his day he could be more productive—finally get his inbox conquered and his e-mail cleaned up. Perhaps he could write that memo or make that phone call that would boost his career.

So the marketing genius asks himself more questions: "Why does my customer want to be more productive? Is it because he wants a better salary? And if so, why is that? Is it because he wants a nicer home? And if he wants a nicer home, why? To please his family? To impress his friends? And why does he want to please his family and impress his friends?"

By digging below the surface and figuring out the answers to questions like these, you will hold your prospect's heart in your hand.

THE USP: MAKING YOUR PRODUCT STAND OUT FROM THE COMPETITION

If you can't compete on price—and most new businesses can't—you have to compete with your product itself. And that means positioning it as somehow *different from* and *better than* other products of its kind. You do that by establishing a Unique Selling Proposition (USP) and emphasizing that in your advertising.

Here are some tips for coming up with a strong USP:

The Best USPs Have the Appearance of Uniqueness

The feature or benefit you decide to promote with your USP does not necessarily have to be unique to your product. But it does have to seem like it is. If, for example, you're a tailor and you wash and iron every item of clothing you mend, make the washing and ironing your USP. Other tailors may be performing those same services—but if they're not mentioning it in their advertising, it will make you appear to be the only one.

The Best USPs Have a Trendy Appeal

The appearance of uniqueness is not enough. If the feature or benefit you're promoting is not desirable, it will do you no good. The best USPs are those that tap into trends. The big screen on Apple's iPhone, for example, is a feature emphasized in all its ads. It plays into a growing demand for bigger and more technically-refined TV screens.

The Best USPs Are Conceptually Simple

If your product's USP is trendy, it is almost certainly simple too. Very few complicated things ever become trendy. And keep in mind that you have to sell the USP. And nothing sells well that is difficult to explain. The FedEx slogan—"When it absolutely, positively has to be there overnight"—is a great example of a conceptually simple (and highly successful) USP.

MARKETING TIP: HAMMER THE NAIL

When you have a sales message you believe in . . . drive it home. And not just once, but over and over again. Take a hammer, a nail, and a block of wood. Hit the nail once, and you can easily pull it out of the block of wood. Put the same nail back into the same hole and hit it six times. Now try to pull it out.

HOW TO USE YOUR USP TO CREATE A SUCCESSFUL ADVERTISING CAMPAIGN

The best promotional copy focuses on *one* Big Idea and *one* Big Promise.

The Big Idea is the main idea you're going to use to sell your product. It comes from your USP. If the USP is strong, the Big Idea will also be strong—and it will contain a Big Promise.

You make the promise at the beginning of the copy. And with the rest of the copy, you prove that you can deliver what you said you would.

The entire process looks like this:

- You make a list of every feature of your product that you can think of.
- You make a separate list of every possible benefit those features can provide.
- You identify a rising trend in your market—a trend that is just beginning.

- You then ask yourself: "Which of my product benefits could tie into that trend?" And you turn those benefits into potential USPs.
- You pick the strongest ones—the USPs that are most likely to resonate with your prospective customers.
- For each of those strong USPs, you come up with a Big Idea.
- For each of those Big Ideas, you create one or several headlines that express a Big Promise.
- You then make a list of all the possible specific claims you can make that are related to the Big Promise.
- For every claim, you make sure you have proof to back it up. If you can't back it up, you get rid of it.
- You write at least two versions of your promotion—each version expressing a different Big Idea—and you test them.
- You take the version that works best and roll it out.

Once you have a profitable promotion going, you immediately get started on your next test. Marketing geniuses know that there's always going to be something they can tweak to get a better response rate—and bring in more money.

RESIST THE URGE TO TRY SOMETHING COMPLETELY DIFFERENT

Your primary job is to sell. It is to convince your prospective customers that you're providing good value for a fair price. For direct marketing, this is the proven formula:

- You make promises.
- You demonstrate benefits.
- You make specific claims and prove those claims.
- You make an irresistible offer.
- You guarantee satisfaction.

Anything else is completely unnecessary. And more often than not, it will thwart the sales process.

It's natural to want to try something completely different. After all, who would be content to bang away on the same six bongos year after year when there is an entire orchestra of instruments waiting to be played?

Resist the urge.

Yes, you want to continually test different copy elements . . . and different offers . . . and different advertising media. But if you drift far away from the basic formula, your advertising will stop working. And if you take the time to figure out why, you may discover that you forgot one of the most elementary marketing secrets of them all: Stick to what the marketing geniuses who came before you have already proven to be true.

SHORT-TERM RESULTS VERSUS LONG-TERM PROFITS

There is a strong temptation for marketers to boost sales by hyping the product they're selling with sensational language. The temptation arises not from their schlocky hearts but from the experience of testing hypey copy versus less-hypey copy.

You may hope that the less-hypey copy will prevail. But it seldom does. Otherwise intelligent and sensitive prospective customers consistently make buying decisions based on over-the-top promises. They respond to cliché-laden language over more reasonable copy.

I've been involved in such tests at least 100 times. And in most cases, the hype won. I didn't want it to be so, but it was. So I listened to the market. I wrote (and taught others to write) hypey headlines and leads for ads. They worked. But I never felt good about them.

Then I started to develop a different idea. The idea came from an experience I had as a consultant with a wealth-building "club."

The club had great, fast success. By coming up with clever products and promoting them to "members" with unrestrained copy, we were able to grow from nothing to $5 million in sales in less than two years.

It was very profitable . . . at least for those first two years. The club grew again the third year but its profits disappeared. The next year, we struck gold with a great new product, and the profits were back. But the following year, there were big losses.

We were working very hard. But after five years, on an accumulated basis, the club hadn't made any money. What went wrong?

One theory was that members were not quality buyers. But when I looked at their actual buying history, I noticed something curious: Many were buying very well during the first year of their membership. But over time, they bought less and less.

Why were otherwise quality customers becoming hesitant to respond to our ads?

The answer, of course, was that we were bringing them in with some very strong promises. But after they became members, things changed. They found us long on hype but short on sincerity. They began to question the value we were providing. Then they stopped responding to our ads because they just didn't believe us anymore.

Despite record-breaking growth, the club was forced to close because it simply did not make consistent profits. I was disappointed to see something that I'd been involved with from the start come to an end. But I was extremely excited by the discovery I'd made: Short-term marketing results don't necessarily determine long-term profits.

This is such an important secret—and is so widely unknown in the marketing world—that it bears repeating: *Short-term marketing results don't necessarily determine long-term profits.*

The reason is simple. Your customers may initially be responsive to bells and whistles. But in the long run, what they want from you is honesty, sincerity, integrity, and value.

Yes, you can make quick bucks by bowling your customers over with inflated claims and exaggerated promises. But those bucks won't keep coming once they figure out who you really are and what you're really up to.

Remember what I said at the beginning of this chapter: You not only want to get people to buy your products—you want to turn them into loyal customers who will buy from you again and again. It's these back-end sales that will ensure the continued growth of your business.

CHAPTER 8

MAINTAINING CONTROL OF YOUR GROWING BUSINESS

In the beginning, you do everything. You answer to no one. (That, after all, is one of the reasons you wanted to have your own business to begin with.) All of the decisions that need to be made—big and small—are made by you. And when you make the right ones, you find yourself in charge of what I refer to in my book *Ready, Fire, Aim* as a Stage Two business.

By turning yourself into a marketing genius and discovering your Optimum Selling Strategy (OSS), you've gotten your business from zero to about $1 million in sales. And now you're ready to take it to the next level: $10 million in sales.

For that to happen, though, you have to come up with a constant stream of new product and marketing ideas. If you don't, the company you worked so hard to get up and running will falter and die. Your lead product, which got you where you are, will exhaust itself. You will have fewer and fewer potential customers.

At this point, you can't do everything yourself. You need help to continue to grow your business. In Chapter Five, I urged you to start looking for superstar employees even before you needed them. Well, now you need them. And a set of new skills comes into play—management skills.

Ideally, you'll have superstars in charge of accounting, marketing, and operations. So now, in addition to continuing to be your company's primary idea guy, you have to oversee what they're doing.

In this chapter, let's look at some of what you'll be dealing with in your new role.

> *"The secret of success is constancy of purpose."*
> —*Benjamin Disraeli*

PUSHING HARD FOR PROFITS

Some years ago, when I was still actively running several businesses, I decided to review a month's worth of my daily task lists. I was immediately struck by how much of my time was spent prodding people. I was supposed to be an idea man. Yet, by memo, meeting, fax, e-mail, and phone, more than half of my working hours were dedicated to poking, urging, encouraging, bothering, badgering, and sometimes threatening perfectly good and competent managers.

There's a good reason for that. No matter how good your ideas are, if you don't stay on top of your people to make sure they're put into action, your business will not make as much progress as it could.

Even now, as a consultant, pushing is a big part of my job. Today, for instance, I sent out, for probably the twenty-fifth time, a memo on a multimillion-dollar product idea. This idea has been bandied about for three or four years. It's a Big Idea and a good one. Its implementation is, admittedly, complicated. But it's an idea that can be (and should have been) implemented. Because this particular idea is complicated (even messy), there has been a tendency to put it on hold. To incubate it.

Sometimes that strategy makes sense. Especially when the idea is fresh and poorly analyzed. In the rush of a first thought, important considerations can be overlooked. If you set aside brand-new ideas for a few weeks or months, you will often discover that they are not as good as you once thought. And so you don't go forward with them. This keeps you from wasting time and money.

Other times, a good new idea is set aside for a while and when it comes back on the table it has become a great idea. Like good Bordeaux, some ideas need aging.

Thinking over new ideas is a good thing. Thinking about them over and over again is not.

At some point, you have to step in and make something happen. Here's how to do it:

- The first step in getting a project going is to appoint someone to be in charge of it.
- Ask him for a specific list of all the reasons the project is still on hold—all possible doubts and objections.
- Meet with him to discuss ways to overcome those doubts and objections.
- Remind him that the faster you can get things going, the faster you can fix the problems. (After all, until an idea is field-tested, most of the problems are really theoretical.)
- Come up with an agreed-upon list of the specific tasks that need to be accomplished. If possible, establish deadlines.
- Finally, rotate this task list through your monthly to-do file so you can keep prodding and pushing the project forward.

This last step is the most important one. And it's not difficult. Just send a note to the project manager once a month asking for a progress report. If he's run into any obstacles, give him your suggestions for overcoming them. File his report and your reply. The following month, do the same thing.

As I said, when I was running businesses actively, most of my time was spent doing this kind of work. It was not stimulating or glamorous. To tell you the truth, it was rather stressful. But it was a very effective way to move those businesses forward.

YOU CAN NEVER, EVER STOP PUSHING ON EVERY SINGLE FRONT

The moment you let up on the pressure to produce, sell, save, and improve, your bottom line will begin to shrink. If you let up on it long enough, all the profits will eventually seep out of your good business.

Consider this:

- The primary goal of most of your customers is to get the most from you and pay the least amount for it.
- The primary goal of the average employee is to get the highest salary and do the least amount of work.
- The primary goal of your competitors is to give your customers the impression that they can get more and pay less by buying from them instead of you.

This adds up to a natural and relentless tendency for your expenses to rise and your profit margins to shrink. It's an inevitable and eternal law of business.

The only thing that can counter that tendency is you: your energy and your persistence.

You can't let up.

Profits are not natural. They are the result of unnatural pressure. They are the something extra that is produced when one person stirs up so much energy that he affects the energy production of those around him.

If the pressure to preserve profits doesn't come from you, it may not come at all.

As a business builder, you are the starter motor that sets in motion a half-dozen engines around you. That, in turn, sets in motion another 36, which, in turn, set in motion another 216, and so on.

Do this now: Make a formal personal commitment to double the pressure to produce, sell, save, and improve. Keep it doubled at least until you have found someone or several people who will apply the same amount of pressure even when you don't.

Now, nothing will keep your profits from growing. And you'll have a new problem . . . a very good problem: how to distribute them.

Which brings us to this question . . .

HOW MUCH OF YOUR PROFITS SHOULD GO INTO YOUR POCKET—AND HOW MUCH SHOULD GO BACK INTO YOUR BUSINESS?

Sooner or later, you will run into the sticky problem of executive compensation: How much should a CEO/owner get paid?

How much you pay yourself is a difficult and important question for most entrepreneurs. Your answer says a lot about your commitment to your business. It involves such issues as employee morale and company culture. And even if your compensation could be hidden from everyone but you, there is still the all-important consideration of how you should be spending your cash. Every dollar you pay yourself is a dollar you can't be reinvesting in the growth of your business.

I've done it both ways and in between.

Most commonly, you face a dilemma. If you take more money now, there may be less value in the business later. Yet, if you take too little, you will feel as if you're working for peanuts. And what if something goes wrong and all those retained earnings disappear?

So how do you pay yourself fairly and leave plenty of money in the business to pay for expansion?

Here's what I recommend.

First, you must figure out what you do and break that down into jobs. If you are the CEO, figure out how much you'd have to pay a CEO to run your company. Give yourself that salary—the same base and the same incentives—but nothing more for being CEO.

After doing that, recognize that there are things you are doing for your company that go beyond what any hired hand, however good, would ever do. The way you care about your company and the ideas you have for its development, for example. These are assets you can't evaluate precisely, but they are enormously important. As Frederick Winslow Taylor, the world's first full-fledged efficiency expert, said (a century ago), "Men will not do an extraordinary day's work for an ordinary day's pay." Recognize this fact and feel free to pay yourself something extra for the extras you contribute.

Then, of course, there is the variable compensation—your chance to reward yourself for your role as investor and equity holder. How much you take in during any given year is a complex question. It depends on the cash flow and the lifetime value of your customers. It depends on your growth plans, the regulatory environment, your competition, and your personal plans.

WHY YOU SHOULD IGNORE THE "EXPERTS" AND DETERMINE YOUR OWN COMPENSATION

There is a lot of discussion today about how much CEOs should make. As an owner of a small and growing business, you should ignore it. Most opinions on the matter come from "experts" who have never owned a business. They have never been offered a million-dollar-plus salary. And they have never had the opportunity to choose between reinvesting dollars and keeping them for themselves.

Pay yourself a fair salary. Make it equal to what you'd have to pay someone else to do the same job. If you have investors, distribute profits to them as often as you can, but never more than is reasonable. And reward yourself for the extras you give the business.

Want more specificity? My hunch is that the total performance-based compensation provided by a business should be around 20 percent to 30 percent of profits. And I believe that the person (or persons) on top should get about half of it.

One more thing . . .

I think your base compensation should be—in profitable years—a fraction of your total compensation. So, if you have a $10 million gross, $1 million net (before performance-based incentives) business, you should be paying yourself a base of between $76,000 and $150,000 with a bonus of maybe 2 or 3 percent. That is your CEO compensation. That would amount to between $95,000 and $180,000.

If, after paying yourself for your CEO contributions, you decided you could afford to distribute a percentage of the profits, you'd get your share of that too.

Everyone has a different comfort level when it comes to distributing the profits of a successful business. With a little trial and error, you will find yours. After all, dealing with the money end of things is something you expected to do.

CREATE A CULTURE THAT RESPECTS MONEY

I like spending money—but I make an effort to count pennies when it comes to business.

For one thing, there are times when your business can't be forced into growth. When increasing sales is not an option, cutting costs is often a necessity. If you don't do it, your bottom line will disappear—one dollar at a time.

Plus, when you spend money carefully, you feel both smart and virtuous. It is just plain foolishness to throw income away on something unnecessary, unplanned, or unwanted.

If you can get everyone in your company to be respectful of money—to value saving and be critical about spending—a surprising camaraderie will develop. People will work together to keep costs down. They will take pride in their frugality.

I'm not talking about cutting salaries and benefits. I don't believe in that. I'm talking about:

- not buying a new photocopier when you can repair the old one
- being willing to switch vendors when the old ones can't be competitive
- reprocessing paper so that both sides get used

That sort of thing.

Profits are the residue of extraordinary effort. If you don't constantly push to make more sales and reduce spending, your profits naturally and inevitably shrink to nothing. By keeping the pressure on—both to increase the top line and decrease expenses—you create something that is the product of all that hard work.

Respect the money your business makes. Spend it cautiously. Reinvest it wisely. Understand what it represents. Communicate that understanding to all the members of your workforce. They are all involved, in one way or another, in the production of profit. It's your job to get a respectful cash mindset in place.

KEEP YOUR EYE ON THE NUMBERS

Your business is growing at a good rate. Every year, you boost it forward by creating one or several new product lines or divisions. One of these products becomes a favorite of yours. You like it so much, you want it to work. In fact, you want it to be massively successful.

There are little bits of evidence that your favorite project is not as good as you want to believe, but you ignore them. When someone criticizes it, you feel defensive. If you get marketing or financial reports that look bad, you insist that they are flawed. You ask to have them refigured. If the reports come back looking good, you are happy.

Love is blind—but you don't want to turn a blind eye to your business.

There is only one way to keep from falling into this trap: No matter how much confidence you have in your superstars, make sure you devote some time each month to critically investigating all the numbers. Don't accept glib answers or superficial explanations. If something doesn't make perfect sense to you, keep asking questions till you get a satisfactory answer.

A second thing you can do: Keep tabs on the cash. Know how much cash you have on a daily basis. This applies even when your business becomes a large one.

Third, make sure you have an accurate idea of accounts payable and other balance-sheet items that might not appear on your profit statements.

And, finally, keep plugged into the sales and marketing activity of your business. When this is profitable, everything else can be fixed. But when it starts to collapse, the business is in danger—no matter what the reports say.

NEVER LOSE YOUR COMPETITIVE EDGE

What do you think Warren Buffett, one of the most successful investors in the world, looks for in a company? It's something he calls "durable competitive advantage." It's what ensures that a business that is doing well now will still be doing well in 10 or 20 years.

It goes back to the Unique Selling Proposition (USP) that I spelled out in Chapter Seven. Your USP is what makes you different and/or better than your competitors. That's what gives you an edge in the marketplace. It's the reason your customer buys from you instead of someone else. And it rarely has anything to do with price.

For instance, it's much cheaper to buy a cup of coffee from McDonald's than from Starbucks. So why is Starbucks still in business? Because they have made the Starbucks experience their competitive advantage.

When you go to Starbucks for a cup of coffee, you're going for more than a cup of coffee. The store looks upscale. It smells great. The beverages have special names. Customer service is superb. You're also aware of the company's high standards. They publicize their social and environmental responsibility. You feel good about spending your money on their ethically sourced, fair-traded products.

McDonald's got some good press by adding premium coffee to their menu, but they'll never have Starbucks' competitive edge. It's what Warren Buffett calls the "moat" around the economic castle.

HOW TIFFANY & CO. LOST THEIR EDGE— AND FOUND IT AGAIN

In the late 1990s, the honchos at Tiffany & Co. made the mistake of downgrading their product line to attract a wider audience. They decided to sell inexpensive silver jewelry to take advantage of the booming market for affordable luxury— that is, brand names that middle-class people could afford to buy. "The 1997 introduction of the silver 'return to Tiffany' collection, which offered jewelry inscribed with the Tiffany name for just over $100, was a huge hit," *The Wall Street Journal* reported.

Sales exploded, earnings more than doubled, and the stock price shot up too. But in the years that followed, Tiffany lost their exclusiveness as their stores became crowded with younger and less affluent people. "I felt like I was in Macy's," one long-time Tiffany customer told the *WSJ*.

Although there was plenty of profit in the low-end jewelry, this sales tactic seriously diluted the Tiffany brand. In 2002, Tiffany leadership finally recognized that and decided to reassert their claim on the luxury corner of their market. They began raising prices on their less-expensive items and, after a lag, sales of those products slowed and their stores became less crowded. At the same time, buying of their higher-priced items started to grow.

Even if it did cost them earnings in the short run, getting out of the middle market was the right move. Tiffany has always had a brilliant selling strategy that appealed perfectly to the sophisticated, high-end buyer:

- Beautiful, quiet stores
- Famously attentive clerks
- A dual product line (expensive jewelry and attractive silver accessories) that appealed to the same wealthy buyer

By going back to that, they reclaimed their competitive advantage.

SET HIGH STANDARDS FOR CUSTOMER SERVICE—AND MAKE SURE THEY STAY HIGH

It's a fact of life that customer service will slowly but surely go to pot if it is not monitored.

Set, for example, a two-ring standard for answering the phone. Spend a week or two working with your people to get them up to, say, a 90 percent compliance rate. Then leave them alone for a year. What will you see when you check back with them? The phone will be ringing, on the average, three or four times and the number of dropped calls will have skyrocketed.

I've had this experience with many companies I've consulted with. AP, for example, hired me to improve marketing and increase sales. But since the company had a reputation for lousy customer service, one of the first things I did was call the customer service line, pretending to be a customer. It was a disaster. The phone rang eight times before being picked up. Then I was put on hold. Mind you, this was an $8 million company. I knew it would be impossible for me to help AP grow the business unless we fixed it. It would be like trying to bail out a leaking boat.

So I went in and revamped the customer service process. This involved replacing staff, introducing a training program, and implementing a reporting system. I hired a manager to continue what I had put in place, and I got on with the business of sales and marketing.

A few years later, I heard that AP's customer service was once again "a joke." I was shocked. And when I checked into it, I was floored. The person I'd hired had left. And the top-notch operation I had worked so hard to set up was back to providing horrendously bad service.

Nothing had gone dramatically wrong. Everyone had given lip service to the high standards I had set. But everyone also knew that AP didn't really pay attention to customer service. He didn't read the reports. He didn't check in with the managers. He neither rewarded good work nor fired poor performers. He supported my efforts to improve this part of the business and had been willing to sign his name to memos that enunciated our high goals. All the while, everyone understood his lack of real commitment.

It was a classic case of what is called entropy—the natural tendency of all things in the universe to fall apart. When it comes to business operations, they fall apart twice as fast if the boss isn't looking. But none as surely and with more damaging consequences than customer service.

Unless you constantly strive to improve your customer service all the time, it will degenerate. Not in leaps and bounds, but in small, sometimes imperceptible, degrees. Only after several years will the difference become obvious.

You can see how this plays out with many airline carriers, hotel chains, and fast-food franchises. Although excellent standards and procedures for customer service have been established, the actual service is often miserable.

This is not solely the fault of the individuals providing the poor service. Equal blame has to be placed on their managers. When you walk into a grimy pizza place staffed by insolent, inarticulate kids who handle your food after sneezing or coughing into their hands . . . you can be absolutely sure that they are *not* meeting the standards established by the parent company. Something bad has happened between the time protocols were established and what is currently happening. That thing is bad management.

The same is true when you get inattentive, indolent, or even abusive service at a Marriott or Holiday Inn. Yes, the receptionist or valet may be a lunk—but the real problem is with the higher-paid people managing them.

I don't think these managers are creating all this bad service on purpose, although I admit to having had that suspicion on occasion. Many of them—in such cases as we are talking about—have gone through interviews and training programs and so on. At one time, at least, they knew and practiced the high standards their bosses want to meet. But because they were not personally committed to those standards and/or did nothing active to maintain them, things gradually and progressively fell apart.

A SUCCESS TRAP YOU DON'T HAVE TO FALL INTO

Hal looked tired. He had been working almost nonstop for a month, running between his office in Honduras, his jobs in Central America, and his second home in Canada. Tonight, he was in Florida, and was talking to me about a development project in Nicaragua.

"You shouldn't be working this hard," I told him.

He agreed. But he'd been putting in these kinds of hours for more than 20 years. His business was getting bigger every year. Yet he wasn't looking any better for it.

We talked about the project. He showed me his plans.

Hal is a very talented developer. He is in great demand in Central America, where his colorful, creative Caribbean-flavored designs have been very successful. And he is an impressive guy—bright, articulate, and accomplished.

He has designed and built dozens of great buildings and commercial projects. With a partner, he virtually transformed a small fishing port on the Great Lakes into a thriving, upscale village.

He's done all that, but he's still working too hard. And—in my view, at least—he's not making enough money.

That's what I thought—and so that's what I told him.

"You started with nothing, and you've built so many beautiful things. You know all sorts of interesting people, have friends all over the world, and enjoy a lifestyle most people can only dream of. Your success has come from providing your clients with great value at very reasonable rates," I said.

He agreed.

"You no longer have to work overtime to get your business going. But you're still working overtime. You have to ask yourself: 'Am I the owner of a valuable business—or am I the most valuable and most overworked employee of a business I happen to own?'"

It hit him right between the eyes.

This is a common problem with people who start and build a business. They do the heroic work of creating something out of nothing. They take the financial and emotional risks, work endless hours to make ends meet, and finally get to see the business grow. Only to discover—late in the game—that the business isn't giving them all they had hoped for when they started out.

What do they have?

- a higher income
- a higher standard of living
- a sense of accomplishment
- more control over the product of their work

That's a lot to get in life. They are certainly better off than they would be as employees. But there are two important things they don't have: more free time and an asset that can be sold for a great deal of money.

Once you've gotten your business past the startup phase, you need to answer the following questions:

- Could you sell your business for a lot of money? Enough to retire on?
- Could you sell it in less than a year?
- If you decided to stop working next month, would your employees be able to run your business without you?
- If your customers discovered that you were no longer actively working, would they continue patronizing your business?

If you can't answer "yes" to all of these questions, you're missing out on one of the primary benefits of entrepreneurship—the ability to eventually cash in on all the work you've done and move on.

It is gratifying to know that your customers want you on the job. But as long as they feel that way, you are tethered to their schedule. If you want to be able to control your own time—to come to work when you wish, leave when the whim to do so hits you, and take long, worry-free vacations—you must become replaceable. There is only one way to do that: Find a superstar who has the potential to replace you as the most valuable person in the business and set him on a course that will lead to that. And don't stop when you find one superstar. Two is better. Three is heaven. Six is ideal. (See Chapter Five.)

In the beginning, the business has to be built around you— your personality, your preferences, and your name. Begin to change that as soon as you can. Begin to make yourself less important. The goal is to transform the organization from one that is personality-based to one that is driven by systems and ideas. This is a difficult challenge—perhaps the most difficult of all. But assuming that you want to sell your business, as a business, sometime in the future, you have to do it.

CHAPTER 9

LEADERSHIP: KEEPING YOUR VISION ALIVE

When Jack Welch took over as CEO of GE, he surprised shareholders and industry analysts by announcing that before the end of his tenure, the flagging industrial giant would climb back from near bankruptcy and become number one or number two in every one of its markets.

At the time, Welch's claim was considered arrogant. But within 10 years, he had done just what he said he would do.

How did he achieve that spectacular feat? By creating a vision for the company—one his workers and associates could be proud of. And by communicating his vision so well that it became a corporate mantra.

As the leader of your company, your vision will change. The goals you work toward as a Stage One startup entrepreneur are different from those you work toward once you have a solid Stage Two business with $10 million in annual revenues. But even when your business grows beyond that—when you're no longer actively running it—your primary job will always be to inspire your people with your vision for the future.

Along the way, of course, many other skills come into play.

Over the years, I've developed a lot of ideas about what makes for effective leadership—all of them based on personal experience and most of them contrary to what you're likely to read in the popular business press.

Let's take a look . . .

"A leader is a dealer in hope."

—*Napoleon Bonaparte*

EFFECTIVE LEADERS MOTIVATE OTHERS TO DO GREAT WORK

Of all the leadership skills, none is more important than the ability to find and nurture extraordinary employees. Nothing will propel a business faster and further.

Great leaders hire the best people, set high goals, make those goals seem exciting, and then keep the entire team focused on the necessary tasks required to achieve them. They are willing to do the hard thinking and come up with innovative ideas. More important, they've learned how to get others to embrace those ideas. Rather than resorting to feel-good incentives (like "Employee-of-the-Month" awards) to bribe their employees to work harder and smarter, they appeal to their inner desire to do their best.

EFFECTIVE LEADERS FOCUS ON WORK, NOT POLITICS

The best leaders are concerned with goals—with purposefully applying their strongest talents to growing the business and pleasing the customer.

They spend very little time thinking about themselves. They're not interested in positioning themselves to take advantage of situations. They don't worry about where they fall in the pecking order—in their industry or in their company.

EFFECTIVE LEADERS UNDERSTAND THAT COMPETITION HAS ITS PLACE IN BUSINESS, BUT IT IS NOT NEARLY AS IMPORTANT AS COOPERATION AND SHARING

Creating an environment where cooperation and sharing are valued is an asset that will repay you in countless ways. When a business gets too competitive, lots of bad things happen. It can lead to unproductive behaviors, such as managers withholding information from each other instead of working together.

I've achieved most of my success in business by forcing myself to ignore my naturally competitive instincts. Rather than worry about how a competitor may be gaining on me, I do better when I think about improving the product or doing a better job of selling it.

EFFECTIVE LEADERS CARE ABOUT THEIR CUSTOMERS

If you care about your customers, you will spend much of your spare time thinking about how your products can improve their lives. That kind of thinking will lead directly to thoughts about how you can increase efficiency, improve quality, expand customer service—all of which will lead to increased revenues.

EFFECTIVE LEADERS MAKE FAST DECISIONS

Business builders are decision makers. They get an idea. They talk it over with someone whose opinion they trust. And then they make a decision to can it or go forward. They know that the sooner they put an idea to the test, the sooner they will find out if it is a good one.

My rule, as you know, is "Ready, Fire, Aim."

Ready means spending some time and serious effort getting your idea "good enough." *Fire* means test-marketing it. If it sells as well as you thought it would, you have something worth marketing on a larger scale. You will have plenty of time to fine-tune it (*Aim* it) after it's been proven to be profitable.

> *"No employer today is independent of those about him. He cannot succeed alone, no matter how great his ability or capital. Business today is more than ever a question of cooperation."*
> —*Orison Swett Marden*

EFFECTIVE LEADERS KNOW HOW TO GET SUPPORT FOR THEIR IDEAS

When you're excited about an idea, you will be tempted to get up in front of the whole company and announce it to everyone at once. But successful leaders recognize that if they expect their ideas to be implemented, they have to get the support of the people who will be doing the implementing.

Usually, that means selling the idea to a handful of influential people—maybe a few department heads, a few technicians, and one or two customer service people. You sell them on the idea by showing them how the company (and they) will benefit from it. Then you let them work the ground troops for you.

A FIVE-PART STRATEGY FOR SELLING YOUR IDEAS TO KEY PEOPLE IN YOUR ORGANIZATION

In Chapter Seven, I outlined the process for writing strong marketing copy to sell your products. The process of selling ideas to your key people is very similar:

1. You identify the biggest benefit of your idea.
2. You turn that benefit into a promise. And you express it in a way that allows your people to visualize it as making their jobs somehow better or easier.
3. You offer proof that you can make good on your promise. ("If 'a' happens, then 'b' will happen . . . and if 'b' happens, then 'c' will happen.")
4. You anticipate objections and concerns before they're articulated. You're ready with solutions for every potential problem and answers for any possible questions.
5. You provide assurances. You won't always have solutions for all the problems. That's okay. Find a way to say that. People don't always need to know how problems are going to be solved. Sometimes, it's enough to know that their leader is confident he can do it.

EFFECTIVE LEADERS KNOW HOW TO DELEGATE

There is something to be said for doing everything yourself—you know it has been done right. But as the CEO of a growing company, you can no longer do that. You have to start passing responsibility on to others. That's the only way to free up your time to focus on the important work of continually improving your business.

There are two things that you should never delegate: the ultimate responsibility for sales and the ultimate responsibility for product quality. But if a project can be completed successfully by someone else . . . delegate it. You should also delegate everything that is beneath your level of ability.

And don't think you should delegate only to someone who already has experience in doing the task at hand. Use delegation as an opportunity to keep your employees challenged and allow them to learn new skills.

HOW TO DELEGATE LIKE A PRO

Strong leaders remain strong by delegating as many tasks as possible. Here's how to do it:

- Meet with the person you've chosen to delegate the job to. Tell him why you chose him.
- Define your objectives. Specify what you would consider to be "success."
- Set a deadline for completion of the job. Explain why that deadline is important. Mark it on your schedule.
- Schedule intermediate deadlines for him to give you progress reports. Mark those deadlines on your schedule and make sure they're met.
- Monitor his progress, but let him do the work without interfering. And make sure he gets the credit—and the glory—for a job well-done.

EFFECTIVE LEADERS DO NOT MICROMANAGE

There are two big problems with micromanaging. First, it is unproductive. It takes up a lot of your time that should be spent on more important things. Second, it undermines the confidence of the person you're micromanaging.

That said, there are times when you have to do it. New hires—even when you hire the best—have to be micromanaged for a period of time. So do experienced employees when you ask them to do new work that only you understand.

EFFECTIVE LEADERS CREATE A CULTURE OF ACCOUNTABILITY

Accountability means that everyone involved in a project feels responsible for its successful outcome—and also for the overall success of the business. The foundation of accountability is trust. You have to trust people to do what they're supposed to do. That, of course, brings us back to the problem of micromanaging.

If, for example, you tell Tom that it's his job to set up a new product-fulfillment operation, you have to give him the freedom and authority (within predetermined, reasonable limits) to do it. If he knows you will be looking over his shoulder, he will never feel responsible for getting the job done well.

> *"Management is efficiency in climbing the ladder of success; leadership determines whether the ladder is leaning against the right wall."*
>
> —*Stephen Covey*

EFFECTIVE LEADERS UNDERSTAND THAT TEAMWORK DOESN'T ALWAYS WORK

The idea that good business requires teamwork is popular these days. And in my experience, there is some merit to it. But only in the right time and place. Fact is, most business leaders are not team players. They like to get things done, but they understand that teamwork doesn't work for every project.

I recommend organizing your crew into a team only for projects that have specific goals and definite deadlines. Like hitting a certain sales target or getting a new product manufactured. Let them know the goal and the deadline. Make it clear that everyone is expected to contribute on an individual basis, but that the goal is to be accomplished (and enjoyed) as a group.

EFFECTIVE LEADERS ARE GOOD COMMUNICATORS

In many ways, leadership is about persuasion—convincing people that your vision, your strategy, your solution is the one to follow. And that means you need to become a skilled speaker. Most people don't like to speak publicly. But the more you do it, the better you'll become and the less anxiety you'll feel.

THREE SECRETS OF MASTER COMMUNICATORS

Secret 1: In writing, and in speaking too, saying less often says more.

Saying less saves you time. It keeps you out of trouble. And it gives your words more force.

Secret 2: Listen . . . and when you're done listening, listen some more.

You don't have to be sympathetic to the other person's point of view—but you do have to listen to it.

Secret 3: Focus on the other person's concerns and interests.

As Dale Carnegie wisely pointed out, "People are not interested in you. They are interested in themselves—morning, noon, and after dinner."

EFFECTIVE LEADERS MAKE EVERY MEETING WORK FOR THEM

Every time you get together with your employees and/or colleagues to discuss business, you have a chance to advance your goals. Like it or not, it is a forced performance. You are on stage. The person or people you are meeting with are the audience. What you do, how you act, what you say, your gestures, and the tone of voice you choose make an impression.

You should, of course, come to every meeting armed with a goal-oriented plan. The plan should include a specific personal goal. ("I will leave the meeting with an agreement from Jeff on the new joint venture.") It should also include ideas about how to attain that goal. ("I'll make a quick, logical argument.")

But if you're running the meeting, you have to do that and something more: You have to make sure the meeting provides an opportunity for everyone else to benefit. Planning a meeting with only your own goals in mind can result in failure, especially if those who attend fail to plan too.

HOW TO PLAN—AND RUN—A PRODUCTIVE MEETING

- Before you call a meeting, decide if you really need to meet at all. Ask yourself if the same work might be better handled by phone, e-mail, or memos.
- Determine what you want from the meeting. Make sure it is an achievable goal.
- Set and maintain a reasonable time limit for the meeting.
- Make sure all the attendees know, beforehand, what the purpose of the meeting will be. It should be specific and limited.
- At the beginning of the meeting, restate its purpose.

(continued)

HOW TO PLAN—AND RUN—A PRODUCTIVE MEETING
(*CONTINUED*)

- Break the meeting into at least two parts. During the first part, the problem or opportunity is presented and comments are invited. During the second part, any questions or objections that were raised are dealt with.
- Be prepared to act like a leader. When people ask for your opinion (as they inevitably will), turn the question around and say, "What do *you* think about it?"
- Appoint someone to put the action plan the group comes up with in writing—with specific deadlines. If the group hasn't come up with a plan, be prepared to put one together yourself after the meeting. But talk about it as if it had come from them—as, in fact, much of it almost certainly did.
- Close the meeting on an upbeat note.

EFFECTIVE LEADERS KNOW HOW TO NEGOTIATE

Most of the deals you make are likely to require little or no actual negotiating. You know what you want out of the arrangement. You find out what the others want by asking. You think about how everyone can have what he wants. And you come up with an arrangement that appeals to everyone.

Getting to that point, of course, often requires a good deal of thought and study on your part. You have to know the issues inside and out. But once you have something that works for both sides, you have the basis for a good and sustainable deal.

NINE SIMPLE STEPS TO NEGOTIATION SUCCESS

1. Learn as much as possible about the other party.

You need to get a feel for who you'll be dealing with. You also need to find some common ground—the deeper issues that both sides can agree on.

2. Set your bottom-line goal.

Ask yourself, if you had to walk away from the negotiation with only one thing, what would it be? Make sure this goal is realistic and attainable.

3. Search for value-creating differences.

What's unique about your position? What's unique about the other side's position? How can you use these differences to your advantage and make your position more valuable to both of you?

4. Face your worst-case scenario.

The worst possible outcome of a negotiation is that you won't reach any agreement at all. If you consider that possibility beforehand—and come up with your best alternative—you won't get trapped into a compromise that really doesn't work for you.

5. Make sure you've met the person/people you'll be negotiating with.

Don't let your first-ever meeting be at the negotiating table. If necessary, try to set up an initial meeting for no other reason than to get acquainted. This will take some of the pressure off.

6. Set an agenda.

The agenda is an outline of the issues that will be discussed. It is a way to make sure that the negotiations stay on course and unrelated issues aren't brought in.

(continued)

**NINE SIMPLE STEPS TO NEGOTIATION SUCCESS
(*CONTINUED*)**

7. Control your temper.

Lashing out during any negotiation is a big mistake, even if the other party started it. If negotiations start to get heated, the best thing to do is remain polite. Listen. Acknowledge the other side's point of view. Then try, if you can, to obtain a smaller, less-important agreement.

8. Learn how to avoid a stalemate.

In my experience, stalemates occur when both sides start focusing on a small issue and lose sight of their common interests. That's why it's so important to keep your eye on the big picture when negotiating.

9. Know how to handle a deadlock.

When you're deadlocked, buy some time. Take a break. Walk away for a while to clear your head. But before you do, set a time to return to the negotiating table—that same day or even later in the week.

EFFECTIVE LEADERS ARE CONSIDERATE

Ambitious entrepreneurs sometimes focus so intensely on their business goals that other considerations—like people's feelings—get sacrificed. They are impatient, critical, condescending, or combative with their employees. And in the short run, no doubt about it, this approach works.

But the best leaders I know don't throw their weight around. They achieve their goals by treating everyone around them with respect. Arrogance and rudeness, they realize, are counterproductive. By putting themselves in other people's shoes to see things from their perspective, they arrive at their destination feeling good about themselves . . . and with better long-term results.

EFFECTIVE LEADERS DON'T BECOME BUDDIES WITH THEIR EMPLOYEES

Good leaders never forget that their relationship with their employees is based on business. That means you don't dump your personal problems on your employees. No matter how stressed out you are—or how open and understanding they may be. And you don't allow them to dump their personal problems on you . . . even if it makes you feel like a hero to provide a solution.

EFFECTIVE LEADERS SOMETIMES ZIG WHEN OTHERS ZAG

As your company's leader, you must stay true to your own vision and not jump on the bandwagon of me-too thinking. It might mean zigging when everyone else in your industry is zagging. It's not safe territory. It's not the middle of the road. But as syndicated columnist Jim Hightower says, "There's nothing in the middle of the road but yellow stripes and dead armadillos."

CHAPTER 10

BUILD YOUR BUSINESS LIKE A GO-CART

Jeff Bezos graduated from Princeton in 1986, with degrees in electrical engineering and computer science. He knew he wanted to run his own company . . . someday. And he had a couple of business ideas in the back of his head. But he also knew that, at age 22, he didn't know enough to do anything with those ideas. So he put his ambitions on hold and went to work for someone else.

In the early 1990s, while doing online research for the company he was working for, he came across the startling statistic that commercial use of the Internet was growing by a phenomenal 2,300 percent a year. His entrepreneurial juices started flowing. He recognized the possibilities, and did some research of his own to see if he could come up with a business idea that would make sense in the context of that growth. What he came up with was the idea of selling books.

He learned that all the major publishers already had electronic lists of their inventory. And he figured that if he could compile those lists—and make it possible for people to buy the books online—he would have the beginning of a business with huge potential.

Excited, Bezos knew that the time had come for him to make the leap. But he did it in classic reluctant entrepreneur fashion. He started slowly and proceeded cautiously, investing very little money until he proved his idea would work. He set up shop in his garage, with extension cords running from the house. His primitive computer stations were placed on tables he made out of doors from The Home Depot.

And that, my friends, was the humble beginning of Amazon.com—what is now a billion-dollar operation with thousands of employees.

At the beginning of this book, I told you that I would help you turn your dream of entrepreneurship into reality. I promised to guide you through the entire process, from having a Stage One startup to being the owner of a growing Stage Two business with revenues between $1 million and $10 million a year. And I said we would do it in reluctant style—by reducing your risk to a minimum while increasing your chances of success.

I also said that we would build your business the way you would build a simple go-cart. I used that metaphor for a couple of reasons. First of all, just about anyone can build a go-cart. All you need is a plan and the right parts. It's also a lot of fun. And when you're done, you're in the driver's seat.

Reluctant entrepreneurship is based on the idea that, like Jeff Bezos, you start out slowly and proceed cautiously. You do your research and develop your business plan. And you keep your day job while you work on your side business at night and on weekends.

In Chapter One, I gave you the big picture—what you need to know in order to be sure reluctant entrepreneurship is right for you. I answered the six questions you're likely to want answers to from the get-go:

1. What does being a reluctant entrepreneur mean?
2. What does it take to manage a side business while keeping your day job?

3. What does it take to make a side business succeed?
4. What common pitfalls should be avoided?
5. Who is best suited for this approach?
6. When, if ever, do you have to choose between your two jobs?

I gave you a mini test to help you determine if you're a reluctant entrepreneur at heart. And (assuming you are) I explained why your cautious nature may be your strongest business asset.

In Chapter Two, I presented the first question you must be able to answer about the product you intend to sell. I gave you Rule Number One of Reluctant Entrepreneurship: "Don't even think about quitting your day job until your business idea is proven and profitable." And I told you how to quickly bring yourself up to speed on the basics of running a business.

Then we got into the nuts and bolts . . .

BUILDING THE GO-CART, STEP BY STEP

Finalizing the Design

There are important decisions to be made at the very beginning—whether you're building a go-cart or starting a business. In Chapter Three, I laid out the six strategic choices that will become the foundation of your business plan:

1. Which industry to get into (And when making this choice, I warned you not to fall prey to the conceit of outside knowledge.)
2. Which product to sell
3. How to add value to your product
4. How to market your product
5. How to come up with the right offer
6. How to get your marketing copy written

Getting Started

Chapter Four was all about putting your idea into motion—taking action. And I gave you three small action steps that you could take immediately:

1. Find a time-management system that will work for you. Getting a side business started will take a lot of hours. You're already working a full-time job . . . so you have to have a system in place to free up the time you're going to need and keep you on track.
2. Figure out how you're going to finance your business. It's never too early to start looking for ways to fund your startup. And I gave you three options to consider.
3. Start learning the ropes—preferably with the help of someone who's already been successful at doing what you want to do.

At this point, you have a solid strategy for moving forward.

Assembling the Parts You're Going to Need

Next, we gathered together the people who will be helping you build, operate, and grow your business. These are also the people who will eventually make it possible for you to retire and reap the full rewards of successful entrepreneurship.

In Chapter Five, the focus was on how to hire employees with superstar potential. I gave you guidelines for recognizing that potential. I also gave you some tips on where to find people who have it—and, once you've found them, how to motivate them to do the best possible job for you. Then I shared my concept of how to structure a company to take full advantage of all this talent.

In Chapter Six, I changed gears and talked about how to create a power network made up of everyone who could make a positive difference in your future.

I included:

- 12 ways to get people to want to do business with you
- How to get your competitors to tell you their most valuable secrets
- Why you should never pass up the opportunity to make a connection with someone—even if it looks like it can't possibly help you

And I gave you a very easy way to keep in touch with all these people so you can be sure they'll be there for you when you need them.

Powering Up the Steering Mechanism and Testing It to Make Sure It Works

Basically, every business is about the selling. No matter how great your product is, you will fail if you can't figure out how to get people to buy it.

In Chapter Seven, I explained why you have to come up with what we call your Optimum Selling Strategy. It's essentially a matter of making educated guesses and then systematically testing various options.

Walking you through the fundamentals, I covered:

- Direct marketing, and why it is ideal for the reluctant entrepreneur (It allows you to inexpensively test different media, products, copy, and offers . . . accurately measure the results . . . and quickly determine what works and what doesn't.)
- The psychology behind the best marketing efforts—how to make your customers want what you're selling
- How to make your product stand out from the competition
- The proven formula for creating a successful advertising campaign—and the best way I know of to learn exactly how to do it (American Writers & Artists Inc. is the

world's leading publisher of home-study programs for direct-response marketing. They can also teach you how to write killer promotional copy.)

Getting Behind the Wheel—And Making Sure You Can Maintain Control

In Chapter Eight, we saw what happens once your business is up and running . . . and profitable. You are now the owner of a Stage Two business, with annual revenues of $1 million to $10 million. To continue to grow your business, you have to depend more and more on the superstar employees you've been hiring. The challenge is to do a good job of managing the work they're doing.

To help you do that, here's some of what I included in that chapter:

- How to get other people to implement your good ideas
- The numbers you must always keep your eye on—even after you turn over the reins to your superstars
- How Tiffany & Co. lost their competitive edge . . . and found it again
- Why providing top-notch customer service is an ongoing struggle

I even tackled the sensitive question of executive compensation. (How much of your profits should go into your pocket—and how much should go back into your business?) And I ended with a warning about a success trap that I don't want you to fall into.

Rolling Down the Road . . . Knowing Exactly Where You're Headed

As CEO of a successful, Stage Two business, you're in the driver's seat. Your primary job will always be to inspire and motivate your people. Along the way, though, other leadership skills come into play.

In Chapter Nine, I introduced you to the main ones:

- A five-part strategy for selling your ideas to key people in your organization
- How to delegate like a pro
- Three secrets of master communicators
- How to plan—and run—a productive meeting
- Nine simple steps to negotiation success

I also said that I have some very definite ideas about leadership, many of them the opposite of what you're likely to read in popular business magazines and books. I mentioned more than a dozen of them. A few examples:

- Effective leaders focus on work, not politics.
- Effective leaders understand that competition has its place in business, but it is not nearly as important as cooperation and sharing.
- Effective leaders create a culture of accountability.
- Effective leaders understand that teamwork doesn't always work.
- Effective leaders don't become buddies with their employees.

It's your vision that started you on the road to entrepreneurship. And now, even when you're no longer actively managing day-to-day operations, your vision will keep the business moving forward.

CONCLUSION

Right now, you're an employee, working for someone else. You have the security of a job with a predictable salary and benefits. But you want more. You have an idea of how to go into business for yourself. But you're afraid. You're not a risk taker.

You bought this book because I promised to show you how to achieve your dream by taking a very conservative approach. An approach that I call reluctant entrepreneurship. I've done it myself and I've helped many friends and colleagues become wealthy by following in my footsteps.

Now it's your turn to make the transition from wannabe to full-fledged business owner.

Are you ready?

APPENDIX

While writing this book, I reviewed many articles and essays that I have written in the past about my own journey to entrepreneurial success. I came across several that I thought would be especially helpful for you, so I thought I would include them here. Most of this material is from *Michael Masterson's Journal*, a weekly blog that I wrote for *Early to Rise* (earlytorise.com). I am using it with the permission of the publisher.

> *"I don't believe you have to be better than everybody else. I believe you have to be better than you ever thought you could be."*
>
> —*Ken Venturi*

DO YOU NEED THE MINDSET OF A CHAMPION TO SUCCEED IN BUSINESS?

Do you have the mindset of a champion?

Are you able to look at your business challenges and feel certain you can overcome them? Do you feel, like Muhammad

Ali and Michael Jordan must have felt, that you have greatness in your soul?

If your answer is "no," don't worry. I don't have that mindset either.

I never did. I never felt like a natural-born winner. I never had the confidence that the people I admired seemed to have.

I doubted I could ever fully understand anything about business when I started writing about it in 1976. Just back from a two-year stint in the Peace Corps, teaching literature to students in Chad, I got a job with a newsletter called *African Business & Trade*. I remember looking at that title on the door my first day and thinking, "What is the difference between business and trade?" I learned fast.

My next business-related position was as editorial director for a small publisher in Florida. I had half a dozen freelance writers reporting to me. My job was to edit and polish their work. But I could barely understand what they were talking about—subjects like robotics and professional practice management and agribusiness. How could I presume to tell them what to do? Again, I learned fast.

When I set out to create and market my own investment newsletter, I was nearly paralyzed with fear. I was not just worried about failing. I was sure I would. But my doubtfulness was proven wrong once again. That publication earned millions of dollars its first year. Eventually, it mushroomed into a $70 million investment publishing franchise.

When I first retired at 39 and spent my days writing poetry and fiction, I didn't imagine for a moment that I'd get any of it published. But in the 12 to 14 months that I did that writing, about a dozen of my stories and six poems were published in literary magazines. Three of them won prizes.

In 1992, Bill Bonner asked me to help him grow his publishing business. I took the job because he made me an irresistible offer. A year later, sales had jumped to $24 million and he asked me if I thought we could eventually be a $100 million business. I remember telling him, "I'd be thrilled if we can keep sales as high as they are. My best guess is that we will get smaller next year, not bigger." But we did get bigger. And when we hit that $100 million target, I said, "Let's just be happy with this." Ten years later, our revenues topped $500 million and our profit margins had doubled too.

When I returned from Africa in 1977, I had a $400 car and about $300 in savings. Today, I live in two multimillion-dollar mansions, have tens of millions of dollars in the bank and brokerage accounts, and interests in businesses with a combined value of more than $20 million.

So I know that you can be successful without thinking like a champion. I know it's possible to accomplish amazing things.

I'm telling you this in case you, too, are full of doubt and fear. I want you to know that you don't necessarily have to change your attitude to be a winner.

I tried to change. I read the books and studied the tapes. I shouted mantras while driving and yelled at myself in the mirror. I did it all, but it didn't change the way I felt. If I'd had to wait till my attitude changed, I'd be waiting still.

Instead, I found something different—a low-key, back-door strategy that I believe will work for anyone who has a humble heart and a doubtful mind.

The success I have had came from two very simple ideas.

1. If I didn't have an abundance of natural talent, I could make up for it by working harder to acquire the skills and knowledge I needed.
2. If I didn't have the natural genius to come up with great ideas, I could find out what rich and successful people were doing and imitate exactly what they did.

When I took that job with *African Business & Trade*, for example, I spent hours every evening in the National Library, studying the subjects I was writing about. I never told my boss

I was doing that extra work because I didn't want him to know how ignorant I was. I simply worked twice as many hours as the other writers. And, slowly but surely, I began to know what I was talking about. Eventually, I was as good as any writer on the team.

When I started writing my first sales letter, I hadn't the faintest notion of how to do it. So I spent several weeknights and weekends reading every successful sales letter I could get my hands on. I copied lines that caught my eye. I made notes about how the sales pitches were structured. I studied how the offers were designed—the pricing and premiums and guarantees that made those great sales letters so effective.

Gradually, I learned what I needed to know. The mysteries that had befuddled me as a beginner in business and marketing slowly became clear.

With each small success, my confidence grew. But it was not confidence in myself. It was confidence in the process of working hard and emulating success.

Years later, after I had built many businesses and acquired wealth, people began treating me like a champion. They assumed I had natural born talents they lacked.

Part of this was my fault. To motivate the people who worked for me, I put on the mask of a champion. I pretended to be undeterred by any problems and happy to take on any challenge.

I now believe I was wrong to do that. In an effort to motivate them, I was doing the opposite. I was unwittingly suggesting that to accomplish what I had accomplished they had to have my confidence and courage.

I should have told them the truth: that my accomplishments came slowly and painstakingly. The reality was that I was a natural born entrepreneurial dimwit. I should have admitted that and explained that my success was the result of mule-like hard work and monkey-like imitation.

The point is this. I don't believe you need the mindset of a champion to be successful in business. You need to do only two things: Work harder than all those who are competing with you and imitate the actions of successful people you admire.

If you do that long enough you will have the success you yearn for. And as a bonus, you will have acquired courage and confidence too.

The courage and confidence I have today was not achieved by mantras or mediation or self-imaging. It was all achieved by the persistent application of hard work and imitation. If you work hard and smart at anything long enough, you will know success. And with each small success, your mind and heart will grow incrementally braver and more confident. Eventually, you will wear the mask of a champion. But when that happens, remember to take it off in front of those you love and care about.

> *"I can imagine no more comfortable frame of mind for the conduct of life than a humorous resignation."*
> —*W. Somerset Maugham*

HOW TO USE HUMOR IN BUSINESS

My friend Bernard opened a furniture shop shortly after he immigrated to Boca Raton, Florida, from Manchester, England, in the early 1980s. That's when I met him. I was shopping for an armoire for our bedroom. Most of the nice ones I'd seen were priced above $500. He had a half-dozen of the same quality for only $195. I asked him how he was able to do it. With a twinkle in his eye, he said, "It's not that my prices are good. It's the other prices that are bad."

Since then, I've bought at least $50,000 worth of furniture from him. And I've seen his business grow from a single shop to a network of wholesale, retail, and manufacturing facilities from here to China.

One reason for this growth is a technique he uses that has allowed him to become very successful and, at the same time, very well liked. And keep in mind that he's in a competitive industry where people are knocking off one another (and suing one another) as automatically as they sneeze.

The Awesome Power of a Light Touch

Bernard is an affable guy. He always seems happy to see you. He asks about your family, business, and friends. He is happy to talk about his life too, if you ask him. And when he does, it is always positive and amusing.

Bernard has a wonderful sense of humor. He is always light-hearted. He is never mean—more Jerry Seinfeld than Larry David. And, like Jerry Seinfeld, he makes you feel that you are in on his joke.

This combination of congeniality and wit is used to make quick friends with customers, employees, and colleagues. The unsaid theme of his humor is that the business you are doing with him is not all that serious. "Let's make a deal," he seems to be saying, "but let's make it fun."

If you tell Bernard you think the price of a particular antique table is high, he won't argue the point, he'll make a joke of it. "For a person of your wealth," he might say, "it is chicken feed!"

If you ask him if he can deliver it on Friday, he'll say, "Friday of what month?" In doing business with Bernard, you can never forget that fighting or fretting about most things simply doesn't make sense.

Bernard has even used this skill to do something I wouldn't think could be done in business.

It took place in High Point, North Carolina, at the annual trade show for furniture wholesalers. A colleague of his who had made a fortune selling designer-brand tables and chairs was furious when he saw that Bernard was selling what appeared to be the very same designer products at a fraction of the price.

When he stormed into Bernard's office to accuse him of knocking him off, Bernard smiled and acknowledged that he had been doing just that. He pointed out that he had done it legally. And then he suggested to the irate wholesaler that he start buying his furniture from Bernard.

"I don't know how he did it," the wholesaler told me, "but he made me feel that what he had done wasn't such a bad thing after all. And somehow he got me laughing. I realized that I wanted to be able to enjoy business the way Bernard does. So I forgave him on the spot, and we have been doing business with one another ever since."

I do not have the skill that Bernard has, but I have been studying his technique for many years. Here are some of the things I've noticed:

- He greets you with a smile.
- He insists on personal chitchat before talking business.
- He never seems to care whether he makes a deal or not.
- He doesn't bargain.
- He doesn't push.
- He doesn't lie.

It is that last one that I find particularly remarkable. In a business that is as competitive as furniture sales, fabricating stories about the value of goods is as common as discount tags.

But Bernard never tells you anything but the truth about his products, how he has them made, and what he pays for them. He is confident that he provides very good value because, coming from Asia as they do, his goods are always priced below the competition. But if you prefer to buy from his competitors, he doesn't seem to mind in the least.

And when Bernard has a tough message to deliver (if, for example, he is dissatisfied with the performance of a vendor or an employee), he doesn't sugarcoat the truth. Instead of shying away from difficult discussions, he seeks them out. He seems to know that he has the power to straighten out problems quickly using his finely-tuned sense of humor.

He does what George Bernard Shaw said he always tried to do: Take the trouble to think of the right thing to say, and then say it "with the utmost levity."

This is very powerful, when you think about it. When confronted with a difficult or awkward business situation, we usually feel that the prudent thing to do is to say nothing. But saying nothing conveys nothing. The fraud is not unmasked. The foolishness is not sanctioned. The reprobate is not reproached.

Bernard's way of communicating—his wit and lightheartedness—is not something one would normally think of as having anything to do with business, wealth building, or personal achievement.

But Bernard uses it every day to handle all sorts of problems and accomplish his objectives.

When it comes to interpersonal communications, Bernard's approach can work wonders for you, too. It can:

• Dismantle tension
• Create intimacy
• Defuse anger
• Eviscerate quibbling differences
• Aid in the formation of trust, and
• Help form deep and lasting relationships

The ability to tell jokes is often thought to be a useful business skill. In actuality, it demonstrates nothing except that you have the capacity to be trivial—to memorize a remark or anecdote and retell it for the amusement of others.

And if joking is bad, punning is worse. A punster's only attribute is a remarkable lack of embarrassment. He is willing to verbalize inanities that others have the sense to keep to themselves.

By contrast, true humor involves wit, requires intelligence, and draws from an appreciation of the absurdity and pathos of life.

Humor is funny. Joking is, at best, amusing. And punning? Spare me.

Leo C. Rosten was speaking about wit when he said that humor is "the subtlest and chanciest of literary forms. It is surely not accidental that there are a thousand novelists, essayists, poets, or journalists for each humorist. It is a long, long time between James Thurbers."

If you are interested in these distinctions between wit, joking, and punning, I can recommend a great movie to you. It is titled *Ridicule*.

It is a French film about a rural doctor who goes to Paris to raise money for his practice during the reign of Louis XVI. But to get the ear of the king, he must first educate himself in the many levels of humor that were popular in France at the time.

At the climactic moment, he is in the king's garden, hoping the king might pass by. Sure enough, the king and his secretary come along. The king greets him, and the doctor replies with a witticism.

The king looks perplexed. He turns to his advisor and asks, "Was that a pun or a double entendre?" The advisor considers it carefully and says, "It was a pun."

The king laughs loudly and the audience sighs in relief, knowing our hero has just accomplished his mission.

Enjoy Your Work, Including the Bumps

If you don't right now have the power to put people at ease with humor, you can develop it by doing as my friend Bernard does: Greet each person with a smile. Ask about something personal before discussing business. And try to maintain a light-hearted attitude—especially if the conversation is difficult.

With practice, Bernard's technique will eventually become second nature to you. That may take some time. (I am still practicing after many years.) But along the way, you will find that you will be able to do business with less stress and more enjoyment.

Humorless businesspeople inevitably become upset when they encounter obstacles or setbacks. They are like wagons without springs, as Henry Ward Beecher said, "jolted by every pebble on the road." What's worse, they are often unhappy even after they achieve their goals.

But with lightheartedness and humor, you can deal with disappointments and surprises with equanimity and even optimism.

"The right to swing my fist ends where the other man's nose begins."

—*Oliver Wendell Holmes*

MUST YOU BE CUTTHROAT TO SUCCEED IN BUSINESS?

"I come from a poor family. I want to start a business and make money to help them. But when I see successful businesspeople depicted on TV and in the movies, it seems like lying and cheating and screwing people is the way to go. I'm worried. Is that what I'm going to have to do?"

This question was posed just after I had given a presentation on entrepreneurship to a group of MBA candidates at Florida Atlantic University. I was momentarily startled by the question. I was sure I hadn't said anything that suggested success in business required a cutthroat approach.

Still, the question was understandable. When Hollywood depicts business and businesspeople, it is more often than not in a negative light. And when Wall Street, the banking community, and the insurance industry screw their clients—as they've done so notoriously—how could any young person think any differently?

So I told the young people in my audience what I'm about to tell you.

It is definitely not necessary to be *bad* to be *good* in business. But the path to business success—and this is especially true for small businesses—is booby-trapped with temptations to do the wrong thing.

I have been starting and growing businesses ever since I was a teenager, and was never tempted to violate my conscience until I went to work for a South-Florida direct-marketing company when I was in my early 30s.

During my time there, I accomplished a lot that I am still proud of. But I also got involved with a few marketing schemes that were misleading. These got me into regulatory trouble and cost me a lot of money.

Looking back at it now, I feel foolish to have allowed myself to act that way. The projects that made the most money in the long run were the good ones. The flim-flam stuff was only good for short-term money. I could have done better had I walked a narrower line.

Most of the successful businesspeople I know are honest men and women who treat their colleagues, vendors, and customers as they would like to be treated themselves. But there are a good number who do cut corners now and then. And there are a few who are bad—who seem to derive pleasure from causing others harm.

I've known direct-mail marketers who bargained with their printers and letter shops to provide service at below cost simply because they knew these guys needed to keep their staffs employed.

I've known owners of profitable businesses who paid lower-level employees minimum wage simply because they could get away with it.

I once worked with a man who refused to pay me my equity in a business when I wanted to get out simply because he knew I wouldn't sue him.

I once worked with a consultant who slandered my client on the Internet as a way to generate business for himself—then had the nerve to teach his dirty trick to people who bought his largely plagiarized marketing program.

The list is endless . . .

These rotten apples prove that you *can* become successful by being ruthless. But if you look at their lives, you can see that their path is not easier, faster, or emotionally satisfying in the end. When you grow your business by being devious, your character is tainted by your actions. You become jealous of your competitors, distrustful of your employees, and suspicious of almost everyone you deal with because you assume they think the way you think. As time goes by, you find yourself spending most of your time fighting to stay in business. It's a miserable way to get rich.

My experience tells me that ruthlessness is not an essential component of entrepreneurial success. Success is always a product of . . .

- Hard work
- Long hours
- The ability to focus
- Marketing know-how
- The will to carry on when faced with any obstacle

Machiavellian business tactics are self-defeating. All those people you suckered will remember you. In their own quiet but powerful ways, they will do whatever they can to see you punished. That may mean anything from ignoring your next sales effort to denouncing you on the Internet to reporting you to the authorities—even to blowing your head off.

Wise businesspeople understand that the trust and loyalty they've earned will pave golden paths of opportunity. With each passing year, every dollar will come more easily because of all the relationships they have developed along the way.

The dozens of good businesspeople I work with these days are open and honest in their dealings, generous with their time and knowledge, and always willing to share in areas of mutual interest.

EP is a great example. We started working together about 15 years ago on some large-scale, residential real estate projects. I knew nothing about that business at the time. He could have easily taken advantage of me in a hundred different ways. Instead, his deals were fair—even generous. He never made a nickel until I made one first. And when one of his deals went bad, he put in a big part of his personal savings to bail out me and the other investors.

When he calls me to say, "I've got a project you might be interested in," I never hesitate to invest. I don't ask to see a business plan and prospectus. I just say, "How much do you need?"

And I'm not the only one who has this level of trust in him. He has established relationships with a group of wealthy investors who are all eager to work with him—even in today's difficult markets.

A few years ago, I loaned one of my Jiu Jitsu instructors $5,000. He was embarrassed when he asked for it, but he needed the money—and I really wanted to help him out. He paid me back every dollar, insisting on paying me interest too. So when he came to me recently and asked for advice on a business he wanted to start, I was happy to give it to him—and to invest a considerable amount of money in the business as well.

Donald Trump presents himself as a very tough businessman. And I'm sure he drives a hard bargain. But I don't think he's ruthless. I've heard from people who've worked with him that his deals are generally fair—and although he can be a bit pompous, his business demeanor is usually measured and respectful.

I have written about Bill Bonner many times. Of all the clients I've had, he is one of the most impressive in terms of the way he treats people. In more than 14 years of working with him, I've never heard him say a bad word about anyone. And I've never heard anyone say a bad word about him.

Treating people fairly is like putting money in the bank and collecting compound interest. As the years go by, your account will grow gradually larger and then, suddenly, it will get huge. When that happens, you can enjoy continued success without working very hard because you will have banked so much goodwill.

One caveat: Treating people well and fairly works for 95 percent of those you come in contact with. As for the other 5 percent—well, there's not much you can do except try to avoid them in the first place.

So before you go into business with anyone (an employee, a colleague, a vendor—anyone), get to know him on a personal basis. Meet him. Ask questions. Ask for references. Check them. If you feel at all concerned that you might be dealing with one of the rotten few, take a pass.

Over the years, I've become a better businessman because I've been influenced by people of good character who were kind enough to give me lots of good advice. Among the things I've learned, I recommend the following to you.

The Ten Commandments of Doing Business

1. The customer is always right. Even when he is wrong.
2. Don't promise what you know you can't deliver.
3. Honor your verbal contracts with the same seriousness as you honor written agreements.

4. When negotiating, always aim for a deal that is as good for your partner as it is for you.

5. If a deal turns out badly for your partner but stays good for you, change it to be fair to him.

6. Always pay your employees as much as or more than they are worth—or, if that is impossible, as much as you can afford to pay them, with the promise of making it up to them later.

7. Share your business wisdom with everyone, including your competitors.

8. Never engage in gossip. Speak as if the person you are speaking about will find out what you are saying. (Because he will.)

9. Never take advantage of your vendors simply because you can. Your goal should be to compensate them fairly, even if it means paying them more than the market demands.

10. Never engage in recriminations and try to avoid litigation. In the long run, it is better to be the *screwee* rather than the *screwer*.

"Mistakes are lessons of wisdom. The past cannot be changed. The future is yet in your power."

—*Hugh White*

THE UNEXPECTED SIDE EFFECTS OF MAKING MONEY (AND HOW TO AVOID THEM)

My life changed dramatically and immediately when, in 1982, I decided to make getting rich my number one goal. But making this change happen had two negative consequences:

1. I gave up thousands of hours of good times with friends and family.

2. I did a few things I wish I hadn't.

When I set that goal, I knew there were more important things in life than money. But I suspected that I would be more likely to achieve it if I made it my number one priority. That turned out to be terribly true. There is enormous power that comes from saying "I will put this goal above all others." It is impossible to understand that power until you have experienced it.

Most people won't even dare to try. And maybe that is because most people have more sense than I had back then.

I didn't recognize how monomaniacal I would become. I didn't anticipate how willing I would be to put my family second. Most of all, I didn't realize that I would be making some ethical concessions along the way. When my partner and I were accused of misleading advertising, I was actually shocked. All of our advertising had been run by lawyers. It was accurate to the letter of the law. How could they call it misleading?

Because some of it was.

I had talked myself into accepting an exaggeration here and there. Individually, they didn't amount to much—but strung together, they manifested themselves in advertising copy that was just plain over the line. Not all of it. Eighty percent of the stuff we did was very straightforward. But that 20 percent got us into trouble.

I regret the compromises I made every time I think about it. So now, when I look back on my decision to make getting rich my number one goal, I feel that it was a big mistake. In the years that have passed since then, I have continued to make plenty of money. But I've done it without sacrificing other important goals.

Knowing what I know now about making money, it's easy to see that I could have made the millions I made—and plenty more—without neglecting my family or getting into trouble with regulators. I could have set money-making goals—even very ambitious ones—without sacrificing any of my other goals or doing something I would regret.

Let's Start With This

The most significant positive result of having getting rich as my number one goal was that it made all my subsequent business decisions easy.

Prior to that, I was never entirely sure if I was making the right call. Faced with multiple options, I could see some merit in just about all of them. I'd force myself to pick one . . . and then worry that it might have been the wrong one.

But once I had established my priority, there was no uncertainty or self-doubt. I'd listen to a question or problem and ask myself, "What solution would give me the best return in terms of money?"

Suddenly, complicated problems were simple to resolve, and difficult questions were easily answered. In a matter of a few months, I was transformed into a marketer who was considered brilliant at coming up with product and advertising ideas.

Within two years of my transformation, our business went from a negative worth of more than a million dollars to considerably more than a million dollars in the black.

And after that, it got better. Much better. It was during that time that my boss/partner gave me a plaque that read "Michael Masterson: Marketing Genius."

So that's what's good about making wealth building your priority. It will give you laser-sharp focus. It will make it easy to make profitable decisions. And it will unleash any hidden marketing genius you have.

If you are starting a business now, you may be thinking, "Hey, it's tough to build a successful business. I'm willing to make the trade-offs you made."

But you don't have to. You can enjoy the immense power of making wealth your number one goal so long as you don't make the two mistakes I made:

1. I was too short-term oriented.
2. I ignored my instincts about product quality.

My partner and I were always going after the short money, as he called it. The short money was the profits you could garner over a matter of weeks or months. We never thought about the long-term development of our business. It was there to make us money as fast as it possibly could. We didn't have long-term plans. We just didn't think that way.

After I retired and came back into business as a consultant, I decided to work only with clients who had long-term ambitions. My first (and eventually biggest) client had absolutely no interest in short-term profits. He was focused on building a business that he could pass on to his children. He lived frugally and took a small salary. When profits were made, 90 percent of them were routinely plowed back into the business for future growth.

That made a huge difference. Key employees understood the company's philosophy on profits and had to be in agreement with them or find another job. Instead of asking, "Which decision will give us the quickest return?" they asked, "What will make us a stronger company five years from now?"

This long-term orientation automatically prevented my client from making the second big mistake I had made. There is only one way to ensure long-term profitability—and that is to produce quality products that customers are happy to keep buying, year after year.

Everyone in business gives lip service to quality, but few are willing to invest time and money to achieve it. Those who do get the golden goose—a business that produces profits more easily as time goes on. Those who don't are condemned to keep running like hamsters in a cage for their profits . . . until they either drop dead of a heart attack or get exposed as the hacks they are.

So if you want to make wealth building your number one goal, go for it. But make sure you go after that wealth with a long-range view of making profits and a serious commitment to creating good products.

If you do it that way, it will be a little tougher at first. You will have to spend more money improving your products, and you'll have to wait a little longer for them to be produced. But in the long run, you'll make more money and you will be happier, because your customers will stay with you and reward you with continued buying.

I was talking to "Eliza" yesterday about her career. She was considering a job offer that would double her income and put her on a rapid road to wealth. "I am tempted to take the job," she told me, "but I don't want to make money the center of my life. I want to do good for people."

Had she said this to me many years ago, I would have told her to get real. Now, I realize that she's right. She should never make the pursuit of money her primary objective. She should be in a business that she wants to be in. She should sell products she's proud of selling. She should find some way to make her business interests coincide with her personal ethics and dreams.

"Yes," I said to Eliza, "make the good you can do for people your primary goal. But pay attention to the money as well, because it will be the best and simplest way to measure the financial health of your business."

You should be in business to provide people with something of value. If you conduct your business correctly and offer them a good deal—and if the product you sell is something they really want—you'll make plenty of money.

One business acquaintance of mine put it this way: "Money is a result, not a cause. If you get into business solely for the money, chances are you will never be great at what you're doing."

That's why so many people fail at network-marketing businesses. They're attracted by the promise of big profits, but then they realize they have to sell soap or vitamins or lotions or whatever, and don't want to do that. Get into a business that you like, learn it thoroughly, and do it right. The money will come automatically.

I've heard the same thing said by professional athletes. The guys who do it right—who have long careers—think in terms of long-term success. They are always practicing to improve their game. They are always interested in learning new skills. They are happy to make as much money as they can, but they know that their lifetime wealth depends on how many years of income they can enjoy, not on how much money they can make in any single year.

Michael Jordan is a great example. Tiger Woods is too. And you'd have to include Andre Agassi and the Williams sisters in that group. There are many athletes who have a short streak of high earnings, but only a handful who enjoy long, profitable careers.

In the world of entertainment, I think of Oprah Winfrey and Howard Stern (an unlikely pairing, I grant you). And Johnny Carson and David Letterman.

These wealth builders must have put making lots of money on top of their priority lists, but they thought in terms of the long run and they constantly worked to be better at what they did.

They worked tirelessly because they wanted to be the best. And in being the best, they earned amazing amounts of money. The money was the result, not the cause.

The moral of the story (if you don't mind hearing it from a reformed sinner) is that money isn't the root of all evil, but the love of money is. Don't love money. Love the idea of building a good business that will last.

Love the good that your business does—the value it brings to your customers and the quality of life it affords your employees.

Cherish the unsolicited testimonials you get from your customers, your vendors, and your subcontractors.

Enjoy the thought that one day you may be able to hand over your business to a child or grandchild or a protégé you care about.

See money for what it is—a neutral indicator of how good your business is at doing what it does, at fulfilling the promises it makes and keeping its customers engaged. If the value you provide is worth the money you get for it, people will buy what you're selling. The better the value you give, the more money you will get.

"Time is money."

—*Benjamin Franklin*

THE TIME-MANAGEMENT SYSTEM THAT WORKS FOR ME

My business life got much better when I started to focus on long-term profitability and quality. But I wasn't able to master my time and get all my personal goals accomplished until I started writing about personal achievement. That forced me to rethink everything I was doing. And after several years of trying different time-management programs, I finally arrived at a system that allowed me to get everything done that I had neglected for the previous 30 years.

The first big breakthrough came when I accepted the fact that I had to manage my time. Until I did that, I insisted I could do just fine by working late at night and expecting everyone around me to keep up with me and clean up the mess I made along the way.

But when I began to set goals and methodically work on them, I discovered how much time I had been wasting. I was able to double my productivity in a matter of months.

The next big breakthrough came when I recognized the importance of prioritizing my goals. I developed a system—borrowed from various experts—that made a huge difference in what I could accomplish. I tweaked this system every chance I got, and it seemed to keep getting better.

It evolved into the system I still use to this day.

Let's say your main goal for the year is to get a business started. Here's how my system can help you do that . . .

Step One: You begin by breaking your yearly goal into 12 manageable, bite-sized monthly goals. In this case, you would determine what you need to do each month to get your business up and running, from doing the initial research to the grand opening.

Step Two: You break each of those 12 monthly goals into four weekly objectives. For instance, if your first monthly goal in getting a new business started is to identify a good business opportunity, perhaps each of your four weekly goals would be to research at least 10 possibilities.

Step Three: You work your way down to the action you will take each day to fulfill your weekly objective. If you have made a commitment to research 10 business opportunities each week, that means one of the top priorities on your daily to-do list would be to research two possibilities.

Expect to spend one full day planning out your year. Once a month, you'll sit down for two or three hours to map out your goals for the next four weeks. Once a week, you'll spend one hour establishing your goals for the next seven days. And you'll spend about 10 or 15 minutes each morning organizing your day.

Daily Planning: Getting the Most From Every Minute

There is no better time to collect your thoughts, review your goals, determine your current responsibilities, and plan your day than early in the morning when everything around you is quiet and still. This is the early morning routine that I recommend:

Get your inputs (5 to 10 minutes)
I start the day by scanning my daily task list, which I have written the night before. If for some reason I haven't prepared

a task list, I do it then, based on my weekly list of objectives. I then scan my e-mails, not responding to anything but noting responses that will need to be made and putting some of them down on my daily task list. I do the same with the in-box that sits on my desk. Finally, I retrieve any phone messages—and if one of them requires action, I make a note of it on my daily task list.

I make it a point *not* to do any work at that point (e.g., send out a quick e-mail response or return a phone message) because I know if I do I'll get bogged down in a lot of small stuff. Instead, I devote this input time to finalizing my daily task list.

Sort and prioritize (5 to 10 minutes)

Now comes the fun part. For each task on my daily to-do list, I indicate the approximate amount of time I expect it will take to complete it. I always try to be realistic in my estimations of time required. Over the years, I've trained myself to be very conservative.

As a general rule, I break up tasks into 15-, 30-, 45-minute, and 1-hour increments. But every once in a while I allow myself two or two and a half hours for a single task.

I like to prioritize my tasks in terms of their importance and urgency. This idea is based on the quadrant developed by Stephen Covey in his bestselling book *The 7 Habits of Highly Effective People.* He identifies tasks as being either (1) Important and Urgent, (2) Important but Not Urgent, (3) Unimportant but Urgent, or (4) Unimportant and Not Urgent.

If we work with this idea, your daily schedule should be focused mainly on (1) and (2) tasks, because these require immediate attention or will advance you toward your ultimate goals. Your schedule should contain a diminishing number of (3) tasks (since they indicate that you are not in control of your schedule), and no (4) tasks at all.

Start with something really important (15 to 60 minutes)

Doing an important task right off the bat gives me an immediate sense of accomplishment that fills me with energy that fuels my work for the rest of the day. I like to make it a non-urgent task, because these are usually the tasks that make the biggest long-term differences—and because they are not urgent, they tend to get overlooked.

This is how I establish my goals, focus my objectives, and set daily tasks. It is not, by any means, an entirely original system. It is a patchwork of systems that have been developed by others and added to by me. But there is something about this particular system that seems to work very well for everyone I have convinced to try it. I encourage you to try it too.

ABOUT THE AUTHOR

Michael Masterson is not your typical businessman. A former Peace Corps volunteer, he never took a class in business, rarely reads the business press, and doesn't like to talk business. But he has played an integral role in dozens of successful businesses—public and private, service- and product-oriented, local and international. As the primary growth strategist for one of those businesses (a former competitor), he helped grow its revenues from $8 million to more than $500 million. Another exceeded the $350 million mark. Eight more have grown to $10 million plus.

Masterson's entrepreneurial experience is immense, even compared to other successful entrepreneurs. He has owned restaurants, bars, nightclubs, and art galleries. At one time or another, he has been in businesses as diverse as information publishing, investment advisories, health and nutrition, sports and fitness, public relations, career advancement, and real estate.

He has written more than a dozen business books. Several of them were *New York Times* and *Wall Street Journal* bestsellers. He has also been a regular contributor to *Early to Rise*, the

Internet's most popular self-improvement newsletter; *M*, an e-zine on entrepreneurship; and *Michael Masterson's Journal*, which reached more than 900,000 readers.

These days, he consults for a handful of private clients and writes for *The Palm Beach Letter*, a newsletter for individual investors.

INDEX